CARL DAHLHAUS

Esthetics

of

Music

translated by

William W. Austin

D0179515

CAMBRIDGE
UNIVERSITY PRESS

Published by the Press Syndicate of the University of Cambridge
The Pitt Building, Trumpington Street, Cambridge CB2 1RP
40 West 20th Street, New York, NY 10011-4211 USA
10 Stamford Road, Oakleigh, Melbourne 3166, Australia

Originally published in German as *Musikästhetik* by Musikverlag
Hans Gerig, Cologne, 1967 and © Musikverlag Hans Gerig, 1967

First published in English by Cambridge University Press 1982 as
Esthetics of Music
English edition © Cambridge University Press 1982
Reprinted 1995

Printed in Great Britain by
Athenæum Press Ltd, Gateshead, Tyne & Wear

Library of Congress Catalog Card number: 81–10080

British Library Cataloguing in Publication Data
Dahlhaus, Carl
Esthetics of music.
1. Music – Philosophy and aesthetics
I. Title   II. Musikästhetik. *English*
780'.1   ML3845

ISBN 0 521 28007 9 paperback

Transferred to
Digital Reprinting 1999

Printed in the
United States of America

Contents

	page
Author's preface to the English edition	vii
Translator's introduction	ix
1. Historical starting-points	1
2. Music as text and work of art	9
3. Changing phases of the esthetics of emotion	16
4. Emancipation of instrumental music	24
5. Judgments of art and of taste	31
6. Genius, enthusiasm, technique	39
7. Affection and idea	42
8. Dialectics of 'sounding inwardness'	46
9. The quarrel over formalism	52
10. Program music	57
11. Tradition and reform in opera	64
12. Esthetics and history	69
13. Toward the phenomenology of music	74
14. Standards of criticism	84
Bibliography	101
Index	113

Author's preface
to the English edition

Esthetics of music is open to suspicion: is it mere speculating, remote from its object, inspired by philosophical ideas more than by musical experience? The example of Immanuel Kant, whose powerful logical thinking led him to esthetic insights that his own experience of art never attained, presents an exception, however, rather than a model from which to abstract any rule. Hegel and Schopenhauer, not to speak of Nietzsche, knew music more comprehensively and fundamentally than some people believe, or affect to believe, who scorn the 'esthetics of philosophers.'

As a whole, music esthetics represents – and this explains some of the resistance to it – the spirit of cultivated bourgeois music lovers, a spirit that arose in the eighteenth century and is threatened in the twentieth with collapse. (Sometimes it seems as if everyone must soon line up with either experts or drudges.) Thinking and talking about music was assumed to 'belong to the matter' as much as practicing music; adequate listening to music was supposed to have a few philosophical and literary prerequisites; these maxims were part of the underlying basis of nineteenth-century music esthetics – and music esthetics is essentially a phenomenon of the nineteenth century.

But the epoch that stamped its character on esthetics of music is by no means a mere bit of the dead past, needing no further concern: as long as the repertory of concerts and opera comes largely or even predominantly from the eighteenth and nineteenth centuries, there is no reason to regard as obsolete and extinct the thinking of an epoch whose works belong to the living present. And this thinking is actually continually present, even if not always consciously so: in the everyday patterns of conduct that determine musical activities, 'esthetics of music' is constantly at work, even if without such constant reflecting about it. Anyone who thinks that reading a libretto is a superfluous bother, simply an annoyance to attending opera, or anyone who, on the contrary, reads the text of a song during a concert, or anyone who ignores the literary program of a symphonic poem as a negligible 'extramusical' appendage to the thing itself, is making music-esthetic decisions whose premises lie in specific ideas developed in the nineteenth century.

Music esthetics, at least that of the present, is by no means a normative discipline. It does not prescribe how anyone should think, but rather explains how thinking has gone on in the course of the centuries. And esthetic decision-making is everyone's own affair. Still, it may not be superfluous to know the presuppositions that undergird the ideas one takes up as a partisan.

A history of music esthetics, in the light of these considerations, is an attempt to understand a piece of the past that is still having effects in the present, indeed every day.

Carl Dahlhaus
1980

Translator's introduction

For 'music' and 'esthetics' (or 'aesthetics') English and German words differ in form and usage only a little, but differences are interesting. English tends to keep the plural 'esthetics,' like 'mathematics' and 'politics,' while German prefers the singular, like 'music,' for all these realms of thought and action. In English nowadays a few of us refer to the many 'musics' of world cultures; a few more of us refer, as the French have long done, to a particular poet's 'esthetic,' reserving the plural for diverging esthetic doctrines or policies. German writers, to make such distinctions, have to go to more trouble. Moreover, German speakers and writers easily collapse the two words, already vague and abstract, into *Musikästhetik*, the title of Professor Dahlhaus's book. German readers need not ask whether Dahlhaus means 'an esthetic of music' or 'the one true esthetics of music' or 'some interesting esthetics of some music' or 'esthetic theories about all music.' A translator of his book is tempted to expand the title to something like 'A systematic and historical survey and critique of the chief esthetic theories about European music.' But hardly for the title-page! My bland 'Esthetics of music' comes close enough to the intriguing ambiguity of *Musikästhetik*. In the course of the book, as in the author's new preface, I often venture still closer, with 'music esthetics,' perhaps more American than British. At some moments I feel an American urge to back away from Europe far enough to suggest that this book expounds 'European thinking about song and dance and their European derivatives.' Will readers permit me to yield to this temptation for the following brief paragraph?

Song and dance are shared by speakers of all human languages, and some of us might say they are shared also by birds, bees, whales, and other species – God knows how many. Thinking about song and dance is somewhat less widely shared. Still more millions of people do think about song and dance than only those of us who use the word 'music' with its connotations from ancient Greece. The thoughts of sages and peasants in China, for instance, might help people anywhere to think about all sorts of music in an age when 'musics' are exchanged via satellites and the old Greek word keeps shedding old connotations.

The word 'esthetics' is linked less firmly with 'music' than with 'philosophy,' as Professor Dahlhaus notes at the outset of his preface. 'Philosophy' may remind us of the endless search for wisdom in dialogue exemplified by Socrates, or more often of the academic disciplines established by his pupil Plato. Among those disciplines esthetics was a late branch, budding in eighteenth-century Germany and blossoming there throughout the nineteenth century, while German-speaking composers were winning glory around the globe. Esthetics deals with painting and poetry and drama and landscape and many other things, so that its dealings with music may neglect the venerable theories and practices of harmony, melody, and rhythm – all traceable to obscure Greek origins. 'Music esthetics' connotes symphonies and their attentive audiences, more than spontaneous singers and dancers. If estheticians claim a scientific universality, this very claim may seem more biassed, in the view of an Anglo-American philosopher or musician of the twentieth century, than the thought of Socrates that philosophy might be the best music. Yet we can hardly dismiss the questions that estheticians have persistently grappled with. No matter how we view them, in whatever broad perspectives, we continue to ask similar questions.

Music esthetics is still so much a German specialty that English-speaking thinkers concerned with music (and musicians thoughtful or thoughtless) owe much to the German philosophical tradition. Our vocabularies may betray debts of which we are unaware. We can improve our thinking by a little study of the German tradition. Carl Dahlhaus offers us an extraordinary concise study of it, based on his familiarity with Kant and Hegel and Adorno, Bach and Beethoven and Schoenberg, together with his vast erudition and his professional concern with composers as far flung as William Byrd, Charles Ives, Benjamin Britten, and John Cage. Professor Dahlhaus can survey the German tradition as its foremost legitimate heir; also as an independent thinker in the latter part of our crowded century, he can help us dispose of any part of that tradition that may be burdensome.

The German words *Musik* and *Tonkunst* are sometimes, but not always, interchangeable. If translating *Tonkunst* as 'the art of tones' may seem pedantic, readers can tolerate it here for the sake of our maintaining a fine distinction characteristic of the subject. *Tonkunst* is associated with *Ästhetik* historically. And in the think-

ing of Carl Dahlhaus 'historical and systematic expositions interpenetrate, for the system of esthetics is its history.' In his own
vocabulary *Tonkunst* has an archaic tinge; the preferred word is
Musik. When appropriate to his argument he distinguishes 'artificial music' from mere song and dance. But much of his text is a
tissue of quotations and the English version may best preserve his
sources' 'art of tones.' Musicians who know some German know
that Beethoven preferred to be called *Tonkünstler* or *Tondichter*
rather than *Komponist*, so here even the clumsy 'artist in tones' or
the dreamy 'tone poet' may be indulged, without any implication
that the music itself is out of date.

German grammar encourages complex thinking. In translating
Carl Dahlhaus, I have tried to be faithful to each of his clauses and
most of their relations among each other, but I have tried harder to
convey something of his forceful tone. The subject of music esthetics, in either language, is not an easy one. But its very difficulty
can be a delight.

Does this book need bibliography and footnotes? For German
readers, in 1967, Professor Dahlhaus dispensed with them, but for
the translation, he has joined me in supplying a bibliography,
including a few authors not mentioned in the text, as well as new
editions and of course as many published translations as possible.
Comments in the bibliography are shown to be either his or mine
by our initials. In the text of the book I have tried to follow his
example about references, using parentheses, but occasionally I'
have succumbed to adding footnotes, for several purposes: to
identify an author unfamiliar to me until Dahlhaus brought him to
attention; to provide dates for a well-known work that Dahlhaus
assumes his readers could assign to a decade; to extend a biblio-
graphical reference when the desirable information would have
made too long a parenthesis. In the references in the text and
usually in the footnotes as well, I have translated titles of works,
with the English first when a translation of the work is available
(German or other original title in parentheses), otherwise original
title first (English in parentheses, to indicate that no translation has
been found).

My difficulties in translation have been alleviated by generous
helpers. Mary Whittall, experienced in translating Dahlhaus's
book on Wagner's music dramas, for Cambridge, and his essays on
the late nineteenth century, for California, has read two of my
many drafts and corrected me on many points; although I have not
adopted all of her suggested improvements, I have hoped to benefit

from them still in my continuing search for *mots justes*, and readers may well share my gratitude to her. I acknowledge help on scattered details from other experts and friends, including Elizabeth Austin, Edward T. Cone, Joseph Kerman, John Spitzer, Dana Radcliffe, and Lou Robinson. The last two helped also in preparing the bibliography and the index. The editors of Cambridge University Press have helped with their many skills. Most thanks must go, of course, to Professor Dahlhaus, for his patience in waiting for me to do the job that I proposed as soon as I read his book, 1969, as well as for his original achievement and for the new preface and supplementary contributions to the new bibliography.

William W. Austin
Cornell University

1

Historical starting-points

If I should succeed in presenting to a student our art's craftsmanship as thoroughly as a carpenter can always present his, then I should be content. And I should be proud if I could declare, paraphrasing a well-known saying: I have relieved composition students of a bad esthetics but given them instead a good theory of craftsmanship.

Arnold Schoenberg's harsh judgment of esthetics, in the introductory chapter of his *Theory of harmony* (*Harmonielehre*, 1911, p. 7),* was well-founded, even though today, more than half a century later, Schoenberg's epigrammatic separation of craftsman's activity and esthetic study seems questionable. In this separation there lurked a danger, now become evident, that the distinction between composers and listeners might be transformed into alienation and mutual incomprehension. To put it drastically, composers may become mechanics, trapped in exclusively technical problems, and listeners become presumptuous dilettantes who believe they are soaring above the situation when in fact they are simply incapable of homing in on it.

The esthetics that Schoenberg dismissed with a scornful gesture as superfluous chatter was a metaphysics of 'the beautiful in music,' misused in journalism to defend an established situation. In the name of this esthetics, guardians of decayed traditions protested against the new music that they did not understand, music that they wanted to shut out of their range of hearing. On the other hand, the craft that Schoenberg contrasted with outworn esthetics meant to him precisely a central core of practices remaining within the bounds of tonality, the very language that Schoenberg had left behind as dead and finished, while traditional esthetics saw in tonality a precondition, given by nature or sanctioned by nature, of all intelligible musical expression. No matter how unceremoniously Schoenberg rejected the norms of a confining esthetics, he was still far from any tendency to subject composing to the rules of a theory of craftsmanship, for composing meant to him inner necessity and

---

* Page numbers in parentheses, throughout, refer to Dahlhaus's sources. Footnotes are all the translator's. The translation of Schoenberg above is close to the Roy Carter version, 1978, p. 12. See 'Schoenberg' in the bibliography.

obeyed only the composer's conscience.

The antithesis of craftsmanship and esthetics, however, has acquired a historical significance far beyond the meaning Schoenberg himself gave it in the passage from the *Theory of harmony*. Whereas nineteenth-century writers on music – even when they were composers, like E. T. A. Hoffmann, Weber, Schumann, and Wagner – were fascinated by the problem of esthetic judgment and its philosophical basis, in the twentieth-century discussion rather focusses on technical questions, just as much among 'neoclassicists' as among 'dodecaphonists.' Robert Schumann, in his essay on the Fantastic Symphony, treated formal analysis as if it violated the spirit of the work: 'Berlioz, who studied medicine in his youth, would hardly have dissected the head of a beautiful corpse more reluctantly than I dissect his first movement. And has my dissection achieved anything useful for my readers?' Today, in contrast to Schumann's day, esthetics is liable to the suspicion that it is mere speculation, remote from facts, judging music from the outside, either dogmatically or according to vague standards of taste, instead of devoting attention to the inner drive peculiar to each work, the 'impulsive life of the sounds,' as Schoenberg once called it.

The tendency toward the technological, however, not only displays the colors of the present, but simultaneously renews the tradition of Aristotle's theory of art, which, since the late eighteenth century, has been sinking in public opinion, though it has never been entirely obliterated. Aristotle spoke of poetic and musical works in the sober language of craftsmanship rather than in theological metaphors. Aristotelian poetics, that is, the teaching of *poiesis*, was a theory of making and producing. The notion of creating was foreign to ancient and medieval art criticism. Thomas Aquinas or Bonaventura would have thought it blasphemy to apply to human works the term 'creation.'

If esthetics – in the proper sense of the word – came to an end around 1900, surrendering its constituent parts to historical studies or philosophy of history, to technology or psychology or sociology of art (various types of phenomenological esthetics that have arisen since the 1920s represent attempts at restoration), then on the other hand its beginnings reach back no further than the eighteenth century. The fact that Alexander Baumgarten first formulated the term *Aesthetica* in 1750 (his fame owes less to the book than to its title) is characteristic of the thing itself. In the strict sense esthetics cannot be attributed to antiquity or the Middle Ages; hence it is no surprise that the discipline that has borne this name since the eighteenth century shows undeniably hybrid traits and is continually threatened in its existence, not to speak of its *raison d'être*. All attempts to define it, whether as a theory of perception (*scientia cognitionis sensitivae*) or as a philosophy of art or as a science of beauty, suffer from dogmatic narrowness, one-sidedness, and arbitrariness, if measured by the disturbingly multifarious phenomenon that the discipline became in the course of the eighteenth and nineteenth centuries. To do justice to this phenomenon requires recognizing that it is not so much a distinct discipline with a firmly limited object of inquiry, as, rather, a vaporous, farflung quintessence of problems and points of view that no one before the eighteenth century could have imagined ever coalescing into a complex with its own name. Even in retrospect the conjunction and interaction of these problems is amazing. Nevertheless, however confusing or even suspect to methodologists may be the aspect of historical accident and deviance that clings to the origin and development of esthetics, so much the more attractive is it to historians. The system of esthetics is its history: a history in which ideas and experiences of heterogeneous origin interpenetrate.

1.

The esthetics of one art is that of the others; only the material is different.

Schumann's aphorism, which provoked Grillparzer and Hanslick to contradict it, depends on the enthusiastic conception of the 'one art' diffracted in various arts as light is in colors. And what made art art, the quality that distinguished art from lowly craft and everyday 'prose,' was named 'poetry' by Schumann, following the precedent of Jean Paul Richter's esthetics.

The thought that art might be a sphere in which an individual work participates, as in Plato's metaphysics a particular thing participates in an Idea, is of Romantic origin: as late as Kant's *Critique of judgment** 'art' means no more than rules to be observed in

---

* Immanuel Kant's *Critique of judgment* (*Kritik der Urteilskraft*, 1790) completes his system, which was begun with the *Critique of pure reason* (*Kritik der reinen Vernunft*, 1781) and carried on in the *Critique of practical reason* (*Kritik der praktischen Vernunft*, 1788). Before Dahlhaus, not many musicians have paid close attention to Kant's critique of music. See Chapter 5 especially.

Excerpts from the *Critique of judgment*, overlapping those to be cited here, are included with a good introductory note in Peter le Huray and James Day, *Music and aesthetics in the eighteenth and early-nineteenth centuries* (Cambridge and New York, 1981).

order to produce a 'correct' piece of work. Moreover, the canon of 'fine arts' presupposed by Schumann, a canon comprising music and poetry alongside architecture, sculpture, and painting, but excluding gardening and jewelry, was only gradually shaped in the eighteenth century.

The distinction between an art exalted as 'poetry' and a craft demoted to 'prose,' no matter how deeply entrenched for a century and a half, is in a broader historical view far from axiomatic. What preceded this distinction was a scheme thousands of years old, which divided Liberal Arts from Mechanic Arts. The old scheme's motivation was different, primarily social, and therefore it led to judgments different from, or even flatly contradictory to, the conceptions that took hold during the nineteenth century. A Liberal Art, such as dialectics, mathematics, music theory, or even playing the kithara, served to cultivate and express an attitude and a way of life worthy of a free man, a man who enjoyed leisure. By contrast a Mechanic Art was a plebeian affair, a work to earn bread, a dirty work, like sculpting, or a work that distorted the face, like blowing the aulos. Vulcan was mocked by the gods, though he was a brilliant artificer. They felt, in the splendor and arrogance of their leisure, superior to his Mechanic Arts.

2.

Esthetic pleasure is essentially one and the same, no matter whether it is evoked by a work of art or immediately produced by the contemplation of nature and life.

The esthetic pleasure that Arthur Schopenhauer means in *The world as will and representation* (vol. I, sec. 37) results from a self-forgetting devotion to Ideas that glimmer in appearances, and the ideas he invokes are Platonic Ideas. (See also le Huray and Day, and Chapter 7 below.) But the metaphysics whose history stretches from Plato and Plotinus through the Platonism of the early Middle Ages and that of the Renaissance down to Shaftesbury and early nineteenth-century esthetics was a metaphysics of beauty, never primarily a philosophy of art. Schopenhauer's word 'immediately' (*unmittelbar*) shows what was primary for him, writing in 1819. If esthetics is regarded as equivalent to a metaphysics of beauty, then, according to Max Dessoir, one can imagine an esthetics in which the very existence of art is never mentioned. Even Kant, at the end of the century of 'taste-criticism,' had developed his criteria of beauty from nature, not art; this procedure led him into some difficulties. Hegel, on the other hand, dismissed natural beauty as a mere reflection of art: cultivating our way of seeing nature is a function, so to speak, of the art of painting.

The beautiful (*to kalon*) praised by Plato in the *Symposium* and the *Phaedrus* is a characteristic of living offspring of nature, beside which the dead products made by men seem pale and vain. Five centuries after Plato, Plotinus specifies beauty as the glimmering of Ideas, as 'sensuous appearance,' in Hegel's terms, meant to express the notion that an Idea shines forth, like radiant light and warmth. Renaissance Platonists like Marsilio Ficino transfer Plato's enthusiasm for living beauty to works of art. Art owes to them its elevation to metaphysical dignity of a secular sort. Yet one can hardly deny that the distinction between Idea and appearance, which Platonism prefers to the Aristotelian model of form and matter, serves doubtful purposes in art theory. For it tempts an observer of a work to turn away quickly from external, perceptible qualities that he judges unessential, in order to take possession of the inner qualities, the content and value.

From the metaphysics of beauty comes the notion that the appropriate norm of behavior toward a work of art is contemplation, self-forgetting absorption in a thing. The esthetic object is isolated, removed from its environment, and regarded with strict exclusiveness as if it were the only thing that existed. Yet the appearance, all too often, is for contemplation a mere route or even a detour on the way toward the Idea of 'Inner Form.' This Idea is sought, not so much in the thing itself, the shape assumed by the spirit, as rather somewhere behind or above the thing, in a world beyond. The metaphysics of beauty, as a philosophy of art, is always in danger of getting beyond art, estranged from art.

3.

The esthetics founded and named by Alexander Baumgarten in 1750 was meant to be a theory of perception, or the 'lower capacity for knowledge,' and it was meant as a complement to logic. Baumgarten ascribed to perception a completeness of its own (*perfectio cognitionis sensitivae*) whereas Leibniz and Christian Wolff had seen perception as only a means of arriving at concepts. The phenomenon on which Baumgarten based his claim for completeness of perception was the appearance of beauty. Thus beauty was not the starting-point for the new discipline of esthetics, but rather

a piece of evidence in an argument aimed at justifying the emancipation of sensuous perception. Baumgarten would show that
perception was no mere preliminary, no shadowy, murky beginning of knowledge, but a kind of knowledge itself (*cognitio*). Then,
since perception had the character of knowledge and the capacity
of existing on its own, there would be in any perception achieving
completeness, fulfilling its assigned possibilities, a multiplicity that
coalesced, a variety of perceptions that shaped itself into a whole.

The notion of the whole is one of the few to survive intact the
transformation of esthetics from theory of perception to metaphysics and on to psychology. This notion of the whole, in the eighteenth century, was directed either toward something objective, as
determining the esthetic object, or toward something subjective,
as characterizing the esthetic condition or esthetic attitude. In
Shaftesbury's *Philosophy of Beauty*, 'the whole' is what authorizes
him to define beauty as a property of objects, and yet to avoid
falling back on the system of rules derived from the sober Aristotelian tradition of art theory, which could only be suspect to the enthusiastic Platonist Shaftesbury. But the notion of the whole
appears in yet another context with Moses Mendelssohn and J. G.
Sulzer, editor of the *Allgemeine Theorie der schönen Künste*
(*General theory of fine arts*): theirs is a context of esthetic-
psychological hypotheses. According to Mendelssohn, what is to
be acknowledged as beautiful must be capable of being scanned
without effort – a claim reminiscent of the principles of Fechner's
'Esthetics from below.' Conversely, if the beautiful thing is to be
easily apprehensible, then its component parts must cohere consistently. Wholeness, thus, is a psychological condition for beauty –
even though this may have been true only within the limits of an
esthetics whose ideal was noble simplicity, an esthetics that in the
name of the simple and natural attacked the 'lofty style' of the
Baroque, which had become suspect as bombast.

The fact that whatever we immediately perceive is not shapeless
but structured has been demonstrated and repeated too often by
modern Gestalt theory. Although in older perception theory particular sensuous traits served as a basis for explaining composite
things, in fact the traits are not immediate and primary, but rather
the outcome of abstracting: particular traits can be specified only
under laboratory conditions, not in ordinary living experience,
where a detail always appears as a partial aspect of a context, of a
'Gestalt.'

Baumgarten used the term 'comparison' (*comparatio, Vergleich*) for the act of consciousness that gathers particular impressions into a complete perception, and he understood this gathering as an activity, not a mere acceptance of something given, as the Gestalt psychologists understand it. Baumgarten differs from Christian Wolff, founder of eighteenth-century German academic philosophy: Wolff saw comparison as a part of reflection, a reflection that searches out common features in a series of phenomena in order to arrive at concepts; Baumgarten emancipated the transitional stage of *comparatio* and made it autonomous, a condition with its own rights, where attention may dwell instead of proceeding through comparison to the forming of concepts. And in fact it is not so much the case that parts of a perception gradually compose a whole as rather, the reverse, that parts are specified from the initial observation of the whole.

The thesis of the primacy of the whole was developed with reference to spatial structures, which stand up to study. Whether acoustic processes, which are 'merely transitory,' as Kant put it, lend themselves to this thesis, and to what extent, is rather doubtful. Notions such as 'trajectory' (*Verlaufsgestalt*) and 'structure of time' (*Zeitgestalt*), which are supposed to bring successive events under the theory of the Gestalt, have not yet been adequately defined and established, either logically or experimentally.

4.

Omnes tacito quodam sensu sine ulla arte aut ratione quae sint in artibus ac rationibus recta ac prava dijudicant. (Concerning arts and reasons everyone judges right and wrong by means of a silent sense, without any art or reason.)

Cicero, writing *On the orator (De oratore*, III, chap. 50), appealed to a hidden sense that distinguishes good from bad without relying on rules or reasons. He was appealing to the capacity that eventually came to be called, metaphorically, 'taste.' In the eighteenth century, such an expenditure of zeal and argument went into the discussion of taste as to warrant speaking of a century of 'taste-criticism.' '*Le goût*,' according to the *Encyclopédie*, is the feeling for beauties and defects in the arts, an immediate discerning, like that of tongue and palate, which likewise precedes any reflection ('le sentiment des beautés et des défauts dans tous les arts: c'est un discernement prompt comme celui de la langue et du palais, et qui prévient comme lui la réflexion'). The philosophical issue of taste was widespread and deeply entrenched, and never resolved.

The concern to get at this elusive, irrational phenomenon with rational means was urgent. Was reason, the complement of feeling, to count as final and supreme authority? Or was taste, the immediate sense for beauty and propriety, to judge independently of rules, often against the rules, and still be right in its judgment? A middle-ground position held that taste – always 'natural,' 'unspoiled' taste, which need not coincide with prevailing taste – anticipates at first impression a judgment that is later confirmed and clarified by the understanding, by reflection oriented by rules; between the involuntary and the reasonable taste there might be something like a 'pre-established harmony.'

Taste, though thought to be a kind of feeling (*sentiment*) or sense (*sens*), was primarily a social category. In agreement with the century's prevailing tendency, Kant defined taste as common sense (*sensus communis*), manifested and maintained in intercourse with others, not in solitary absorption in a work of art. The individual rises, when he shows taste, above the limits of his accidental inclinations. The particular and the universal, the private and the public interpenetrate and interact, yet taste still keeps the quality of a sentiment that is not open to dispute.

There seem to be four aspects characteristic of taste as it was understood in the eighteenth century. First, it always judges over an individual thing, which it takes as a special case conditioned by its particular situation.

Second, more decisive than the individual work or the spectator's extraordinary esthetic condition, to which the work transports him, is the esthetic education and culture (*Bildung und Kultur*) transmitted through art. Third, taste makes negative judgments more often than positive; a choice of what is appropriate results from rejection of what is tasteless, not the reverse. Fourth, taste claims universal validity, even though its object is a particular thing. Yet the universal common sense that legitimizes individual judgment is not so much a fact as a postulate – a 'regulative idea,' to use Kant's term. Judgments of taste, in the imperfect reality we inhabit, very often disagree, and we have no norms that would enable us to demonstrate which judgments are true and false, as we prove mathematical theorems. Yet in judgments of beauty – as distinct from judgments of what is merely pleasant – there is always a claim to universality, explicit or implicit: I may say that a thing is pleasant 'to me' but not that it is beautiful 'to me'; I am impelled by language, which is 'objective spirit,' to claim the agreement of others with my judgment. The court of appeal, however, that should confirm my claim, is not 'men' as a number to be counted, but 'mankind,' which everyone contains in himself, even if only as an undeveloped possibility. 'Asking around,' taking a cue from others, and estimating a public opinion whose shades of gray result from the mutual dependence of inconclusive preferences – all this was contemptible to Kant, despite his philanthropic sentiments. Still he was convinced, nonetheless, that it would not be superfluous to compare his judgments of art works with those of others or with his own earlier judgments, in order to gain distance from himself and his situation. While 'empirical universality,' the agreement of the majority, represents no guarantee of truth, for a prevailing opinion is apt to rest on bedazzlement, such agreement should not be neglected, for it is some indication of the 'ideal universality' of common sense and an antidote to an individual's limitation in himself; the individual's esthetic conscience represents 'mankind' potentially, but not always actually, and it is the ideas of 'mankind' that justify the claim of any judgment of taste to universal validity. A subjective judgment is not yet objective, but it ought to become so. Esthetics, even for the cautious Kant, is tinged with Utopia.

2

Music as text and work of art

Painting works in space and through an artificial presentation of space. Music and all energetic arts work in time, not merely in but also through temporal sequence by means of an artificial temporal exchange of tones. As for poetry, may we not bring its essence within a similar general concept, since poetry works on the soul through arbitrary signs, through the meaning of words? We propose to call the medium of this working 'force.' Then, just as space, time, and force are three basic concepts of metaphysics and just as all mathematical sciences may be traced back to one of these concepts, so we will say also in the theory of fine arts and sciences: those arts that supply works do their work in space; arts that work through energy work in the sequence of time; the fine sciences, or rather the one and only fine science, poetry, works through force.

Johann Gottfried von Herder's sentences defining music as art of
time, said to work 'not merely in but also through temporal
sequence,' come from his 'Erstes kritisches Wäldchen' ('First critical grove,' 1769, *Sämtliche Werke*, vol. III, p. 137), which is his
response to Lessing's *Laokoon* (1766). Herder took over Lessing's
program of defining the arts by means of their characteristic limi-
tations, each art distinct from the others. The tradition behind both
authors was that of Aristotle. Herder shared with Lessing the aim
of developing a theory of the arts, not a metaphysics of beauty.
And Herder used, moreover, the Aristotelian distinction between
making (*poiesis*) and doing (*praxis*), which implicitly underlies the
specification of music in the sentences quoted here. *Poiesis*, understood according to sober Greek usage, means nothing but producing, while *praxis* means practicing and performing acts. When
Herder calls music an 'energetic' art (*energische Kunst*), he means
that it is essentially activity (*energeia*), not a product, a piece of
work (*ergon*). Herder's thought makes applicable to music what
Humboldt said about language, in his essay, 'Über die Verschiedenheit des menschlichen Sprachbaues' ('On the diversity of
human languages and their influence on the intellectual development of the human race,' sec. 12):

Language, grasped in its real essence, is something continual and passing
on in every moment. Even its fixing by means of writing always preserves
it only incompletely, like a mummy; writing stands in need, again and
again, of people's efforts to imagine from writing a living performance.
Language itself is no work (*ergon*) but an activity (*energeia*). Its true definition, therefore, can only be genetic.

Hence, the idea that music is exemplified in works, no matter how
firmly rooted it has become in the past century and a half, is far
from self-evident. The beginnings of this idea extend back into the
sixteenth century. The church musician (*Cantor*) Nicolaus Listenius, who had studied in Wittenberg and submitted to the influence
of Melanchthon, counted composing as a kind of *poiesis* in his treatise of 1537, *Musica*. He separated *musica poetica* from *musica practica* – musical activity – for *musica poetica* was making and
producing, a labor by which something was brought into the world
that would represent, even after its author's death, a complete
work, enduring in its own right. ('Poetica ... consistit enim in
faciendo sive fabricando, hoc est, in labore tali, qui post se etiam
artifice mortuo opus perfectum et absolutum relinquat.') Listenius
puts the accent on the musical text, not the performance. What is

notated is no longer a mere proposal or prescription for 'setting music to work,' but rather is a work itself.

Listenius's notion, however, that music might be an *opus absolutum*, a work in itself, freed from its sounding realization in any present moment, suffused only around 1800 into the consciousness of 'connoisseurs and amateurs.' Even up to the present time this idea is foreign to listeners who restrict their musical experience to popular music. And we would be blind captives of a habit of speaking were we to minimize the resistances met by this idea and pass over them lightly. It can hardly be denied that music is an 'energetic' art, as Herder said (a 'performing art' in some twentieth-century usages). Such an art fulfills itself in activity. Music's existence in the guise of an author's works is problematical.

Music is transitory. It goes by, instead of holding still for inspection. Because of its perishable, fleeting nature, music was conceived by Adam of Fulda, in 1490, as a meditation on death, *meditatio mortis*. If the typical traits of a work of art are, as Bonaventura formulated them, to be beautiful, useful, and solid, then of course music may be, by virtue of its form and its power over affections, an *opus pulchrum et utile*, but not *opus stabile*. The same thought recurs half a millennium later in Hegel's *Aesthetics* – the idea that the temporal structure of music is a deficiency (see le Huray and Day, and Chapter 8 below). Hegel, to be sure, allows to musical works of art 'the beginning of a distinction between an enjoying subject and an objective work,' but Hegel denies that this contrast reaches the point, 'as in the plastic arts, of enduringly, externally maintaining itself in space, available for viewing as an objectivity existing in its own right'; rather 'on the contrary, its real existence' evanesces in 'its own immediate temporal passing' (*Ästhetik*, ed. F. Bassenge, vol. II, p. 275). For Hegel the fact that music is a process, not a lasting thing, is enough to grant it only a slight, vanishing degree of objectivity. Audible things are sensed not as things out there, but rather as events surrounding us and invading us, instead of keeping their distance from us. Kant accused music of lacking urbanity because it obtrudes itself.

Yet rigorously to deny music all 'objectivity on its own' would be erroneous too. Like a work of plastic art, music is also an esthetic object, a focus of esthetic contemplation. However, its objectivity is displayed not so much immediately as indirectly: not in the moment when it is sounding, but only if a listener, at the end of a movement or section, reverts to what has passed and recalls it into his present experience as a closed whole. At this point, music

assumes a quasi-spatial form (Gestalt). What has been heard soli-
difies into something out there, an 'objectivity existing on its own.'
And nothing would be farther from the truth than to see in the tendency to spatialization a distortion of music's nature. Insofar as
music is form, it attains its real existence, paradoxically expressed,
in the very moment when it is past. Still held firm in memory, it
emerges into a condition that it never entered during its immediate
presence; and at a distance it constitutes itself as a surveyable
plastic form. Spatialization and form, emergence and objectivity,
are interdependent: one is the support or precondition of the other.

Since music is essentially activity, *energeia*, as Herder puts it,
music's recording in notation fulfills a different function from the
writing down of language. (Thrasybulos G. Georgiades has
explored the difference.) Fixing music in a text, a composition, is
historically a late phenomenon. In literature too, of course, a leap
separates reciting from writing, or telling a tale from fixing a narra-
tive in a book. Yet written speech represents speech to a greater
extent than notated music represents music. To grasp the meaning
of a literary work, a reader need not bring to mind the phonetic
form of the words, nor even know that form. Through the written
characters, even if a reader dispenses with imaginative completion
of sonorous coloring and speech-gesture, or, with dead languages,
is forced to forgo them, still the meaning is transmitted – not quite
intact but in its basic features. With music, on the contrary, silent
reading, insofar as it is not to collapse into thin abstraction, always
represents an inner hearing, translating signs into sound. Musical
meaning, in contrast to linguistic meaning, is only to a slight extent,
if at all, detachable from the sounding phenomena. To become musically real, a composition needs interpretation in sound.

Nevertheless, it would be an exaggeration to deprive written
music of the status of a text, in the undiluted sense of the word, and
to see in notation nothing but a set of instructions for musical practice. The meaning of music can be specified – in a crude oversimplification that neglects emotional characteristics – as inner
coherence of the relations among the tones constituting a work.
Tone-relations and tone-functions, however, are a third aspect,
extending over and beyond both notation and its realization in
sound. The musical fact that a G major and a C major triad function as dominant and tonic, forming a cadence, a point of repose, is
contained as such neither in the notation nor in the sounding
phenomena. Musical meaning is 'intentional'; it exists only insofar
as a listener grasps it.

Is the meaning of music to be read more easily from notation or from sound? This question has no firm answer *a priori*. Music does not divulge all its meanings in performance. While compositions in which tone-color plays an important role, or even a constitutive role, depend very much on acoustical realizations, still it is undeniable that elaborate motivic relationships often disclose themselves with less trouble to a reading of the music, which is made complete by imagining the sound. And the opinion that only what is audible has any right to musical existence is a questionable prejudice. The difference between written speech and notated music – between the echo of living speech in reading a literary work and the imagination of sound in reading a score – is a difference of degree, not of principle. In opposition to tendencies to deny or minimize the contribution of visual experience toward the understanding of musical works of art, an apology for 'paper music' would be in order.

'The supreme reality of art,' says Walter Benjamin in his *Origin of the German tragic drama,'* 'is isolated, self-contained work.' The concept of a work formed the center around which classical esthetics circled. The age of art-religion, as Heine called it, had a theory of art, formulated in exemplary fashion by Karl Philipp Moritz, in his essay *Von der bildenden Nachahmung des Schönen (On the plastic imitation of the beautiful*, 1788). This theory aimed at something complete and perfect in itself. A structure that makes a claim to the status of art does not exist for the sake of its effect, but rather for the sake of its own inner perfection. As a work of art in the emphatic sense, it is an individual thing, enduring in itself. Moreover, metaphysical value is ascribed to such a work, most unreservedly in Schelling's *Philosophy of art*. Neither the activity whereby it is produced nor the effect that it produces can be decisive in this view, but rather the work's existence in itself. It appears as *opus perfectum et absolutum* in a sense not suspected by the provincial sixteenth-century cantor who originated the formula. Such a work demands of listeners contemplation, self-forgetting study.

The polemical point of the idea that a work of art resided in and endured in itself was directed against the older traditional idea, which had come to be taken for granted, that an *opus pulchrum* was at the same time an *opus utile*; according to the tradition, a work of beauty fulfilled a purpose either practical or moral. Art-religion meant an emancipation of art from religion. Works of art have become detached from any function. For, insofar as a work is a whole in itself, it cannot be part of a more comprehensive whole to which it subjects itself as subservient.

For medieval thinkers, whose ideas continued to exert some effect in Germany up to the early eighteenth century, musical practice, including composition, counted as *ars mechanica*, as technique. This art was measured according to the purposes, religious or secular, that it aimed to serve. Although the numerical proportions forming the basis of musical intervals and rhythms formed the object of a speculative knowledge that kept its validity as *ars liberalis* and as *musica* in the narrower, more exalted sense of the word, practical execution counted among the merely mechanical accomplishments. But the technological viewpoint was not strictly separated from the metaphysical; speculation intervened in practice with rules and also took the sounding phenomena as points of departure, in order to ascend in thinking step by step toward meditating on numerical structures and their meaning. In the thirteenth century, the art of composing a motet was still a handicraft, but at the same time the numbers that ruled rhythms were interpreted allegorically: triple meter, as a perfect measure of time, as *perfectio*, was a symbol of the Holy Trinity. And when the fourteenth-century theorist Jacob of Liège protested against the duple rhythms of *Ars nova*, in his *Speculum musicae* (*Mirror of music*), his objection was motivated in no small part by theology.

Since the eighteenth century, on the contrary, music as art has been separated from handicraft by a gulf that may be felt as a misfortune but cannot be denied. A composer who promotes handicraft in an archaicizing way* may find security in 'setting tones' as if they were 'bricks' but pays for it with a relapse into a second kind of primitivism. Esthetics – the theory of works of art in the modern, emphatic sense – has freed itself both from technological views of music and from speculative and moralizing views. Allegorical interpretations are in disrepute; moral postulates are rejected as intrusions from outside, foreign to art; instructions in craft and recipe books of *musica practica*, ever since Fux's *Gradus ad Parnassum*, have been sinking more and more into mere exercises in a dead language, to studies that of course transmit some concept of disciplined musical grammar, but fall short of real composing. The artificer, formerly an artisan, promotes himself to the status of 'tone poet.'

The functionlessness or autonomy of musical works of art, their emancipation from external goals, means no such radical break with the tradition of functional music, however, as might be sup-

---

* Like Hindemith sometimes.

posed from the bitterness of the polemics which were intended to establish the modern concept of art. The purposes were 'transcended': put out of commission, and at the same time assumed into the interior of the works. Traits that had earlier been imposed on a musical genre from outside transformed themselves into immanent characteristics. The function of the polonaise or mazurka, namely, to serve as dance music for aristocrats or peasants, clung to them even after Chopin stylized them into concert pieces, as emotional coloring and as images in memory or fantasy of long-ago festivities. Kant's specification of beauty as 'purposive without purpose' contains a meaning that he never intended in his *Critique of judgment*: that purposes are indeed expunged as external features but preserved as traits of character.

The transition to autonomy, the emancipation from imposed purposes, was bound up with a reversal of the rankings of individual works and their genres. This reversal occurred gradually: it was prepared almost imperceptibly at first, in the sixteenth century, but then around 1800 emerged unmistakably. In older, functional music, a work was primarily an example of a genre, as an individual person fits into a succession of generations that extends far beyond him and survives him. A work formed not so much an isolated, closed whole, an individuality enduring in itself, as, rather, it exemplified a type, feeding on the historical substance of this type, which had developed in the course of decades or even centuries, and requiring listeners to connect the work with the type in order to understand it. Thus, if a piece of music bore the title 'Barcarole,' it was at least as important, as Ernst Bloch has noticed, that the piece conspicuously represent the type, barcarole, as that it be an individual work with its definite, unrepeatable characteristics.

But since the late eighteenth century all genres have rapidly lost substance. In Chopin's Barcarole (although even this piece invokes a picture of Venice) the peculiar, unrepeatable features are more essential than any general qualities that it shares with other pieces of the same name. The concept of a genre is no longer established in advance for individual works. Rather, every genre fades to an abstract generalization, derived from individual structures after they have accumulated; and finally, in the twentieth century, individual structures submit only under duress to being allocated to any genre.

3

Changing phases of the esthetics of emotion

The ultimate purpose of the various minglings and linkings of tones achieved by art is, by means of their various impacts on the sense mechanisms of hearing, to absorb a listener's whole heart, to keep occupied all the heart's powers, and to nourish its inner well-being through the purification of passions and affections.

Christoph Nichelmann, harpsichordist alongside Carl Philipp Emanuel Bach at the court of Frederick the Great, was an eclectic, who assembled the reigning ideas of the century of Enlightenment in the remarks on esthetics in his book, *Die Melodie nach ihrem Wesen sowohl, als nach ihren Eigenschaften (Melody according to its essence as well as its characteristics*, 1755, chap. XI). Nichelmann was indifferent to either agreement or implicit disagreement among these ideas. An impact or stirring (*Rührung*) – some sort of sensuous–psychic motion or agitation (*Bewegung*) – was the effect demanded from music, especially from clavichord playing, by eighteenth-century sentimentalists. Tears – though short-lived – flowed without shame, and just as little embarrassment was attached, on the other hand, to speaking of the machinery, the 'mechanisms,' that transmitted the pleasure of being stirred. People took a rational attitude toward irrational experience.

Aristotelian catharsis – purification of passions and affections – is both like and unlike the new esthetic emotion; reduced to a means of maintaining the heart's 'well-being,' the purifying process blends, in Nichelmann's esthetic reflections, with Abbé Dubos's haughty aristocratic conviction that boredom is the worst of evils, so that music's 'ultimate purpose' is to banish boredom and 'keep occupied all the heart's powers.' The older doctrine of affections (*Affektenlehre*: cf. *affetti, affettuoso*, etc.) had always bowed to the priority of moral purpose. According to the sixteenth-century Spanish philosopher Juan Luis Vives, in his treatise *De anima* Bk III, affections were excitations moving us to strive for what is good and useful, and to avoid what is bad and harmful.

16

Istarum facultatum quibus animi nostri praediti a natura sunt ad sequen-
dum bonum vel vitandum malum actus dicuntur affectus sive affectiones,
quibus ad bonum ferimur vel contra malum vel a malo recedimus.

Dubos, although a cleric, was more lenient. In his view the direction of feelings was less important than the vigor of excitations that
would heal the illness of boredom. Dubos explained, in his *Critical
reflections (Réflexions critiques*, 1719), that movements of the
heart were ends in themselves. Thus, well before Rousseau, he
established esthetic sentimentalism as a complement to the
century's rationalism. Instead of judgment 'by the path of analysis'
there was to be a valid judgment 'by the path of sentiment.'

The idea that music's goal was to represent and arouse affections
is a commonplace, rooted as deeply in history as the opposing
thesis that music is sounding mathematics. Invoking the authority
of ancient traditions, Isidor of Seville in the seventh century proclaimed: 'Music moves affections and calls forth feelings into a different disposition.' (Musica movet affectus, provocat in diversum
habitum sensus.) And two centuries later Hrabanus Maurus repeated the saying that music moves affections and transports a listener into changing conditions of the heart. Music that does not stir
the passions is mere dead sound.

The doctrine of affections, however, much as it emphasized the
effect of music and the moving of the heart, implicitly presupposed
a conception of the character of musical feelings that was primarily
objective and objectifying. With music before about 1750 it is misleading (or at least liable to misunderstanding) to apply language
that became conventional in the nineteenth century – 'expression'
or 'mood.' The term 'expression' suggests a subject behind the
work, speaking about himself in the musical 'language of feeling.'
Likewise the word 'mood' suggests a complex of feelings in which a
listener is submerged, turned in on his own condition. But the
characters of musical feelings are primarily conceived as objective;
this has been demonstrated by Kurt Huber, in *Der Ausdruck musikalischer Elementarmotive* (*The expression of elementary musical
motives*, 1923).* Involuntarily, listeners attribute an impression of
something serious, sad, or dull to the tonal structure itself as one of
its characteristics. In unprejudiced perception, a melodic motive
does not express dullness and transport one into a dull mood, but
rather it seems dull in itself. Only later, if at all, will anyone experi-

---

* Kurt Huber (1893–1943) pursued professional interests in psychology and folksong research. A participant in the 'White Rose' resistance effort of 1943, he was
  executed by the Nazis.

ence the objective emotional impression as a mere condition or interpret the impression as a sign. Both the transition into a mood felt by a listener as being his own and also the idea that the emotional character must express that of some person, some subject behind the music, are secondary. To be sure, there is no sharp separation of the various aspects. Often they flow into each other imperceptibly. What is at stake can be only an emphasis, not an exclusive domination of one function or another. Yet the change in emphasis is important enough to distinguish one epoch from another in the development of the esthetics of emotion.

Linguistics distinguishes three functions of sentences, according to Karl Bühler: 'triggering,' 'representation,' and 'testimony.' Actions are triggered; states of affairs are represented; conditions of the heart are attested. Now an analogous distinction of functions might be useful in music esthetics, because the doctrine of affections and the esthetics of emotion risk wearing themselves out in monotonous repetitions of the formula that music is 'expression.' The idea of expression has become so ambiguous, vague, and all-encompassing as a slogan in popular esthetics that to rescue it for serious use requires sharpening it and narrowing it down. And the etymology of the word suggests that 'expression' means nothing else than 'testimony,' in the sense in which Wilhelm Heinse explained music as a means of 'relieving one's feelings' and 'letting one's passions gush.' In this narrowed sense, 'esthetics of expression' would not apply to the ancient and medieval doctrine of affections. Affections were 'moved,' according to Isidor; that is, 'triggered' rather than 'attested.' And even ways of speaking that were conventional in the seventeenth and early eighteenth centuries, about music's purpose of 'expressing affections' (*affectus exprimere*), would be misunderstood if the term 'expression' led to thoughts of the composer's or performer's testifying to his emotional excitement. Affections were represented, portrayed, but not 'dredged up from the soul,' not thrust forth from the agitated inner being.

1.

Complexus effectuum musices (The compass of the effects of music) is the title of a treatise by Johannes Tinctoris from the late fifteenth century, comprising speculations and anecdotes accumulated in the course of centuries or even millennia. It celebrates everyday effects alongside miraculous ones: music banishes melancholy, softens a hard heart, exalts to ecstasy or pious contemplation, stimulates to elation or attunes to wisdom. The 'marvelous effects' (*meravigliosi effetti*) that music exerted in antiquity aroused envy among Italian humanists of the sixteenth and seventeenth centuries; their reverence for the ancients held them back from the consoling thought that intensity must sometimes be paid for with primitivity. The concept of effect (*effectus*) is not simple. Tones, understood as stimuli in a physiological–psychological sense, release reflexes; they stimulate feelings that a listener does not objectify but rather feels immediately as his own, as invasions of his heart. He feels exposed to music, instead of beholding it from an esthetic distance. And according to the norms of nineteenth-century esthetics, such a primitive listening, lacking objectivity, is pre-musical – 'pathological' in the sense of self-abandon, of being beside oneself (Eduard Hanslick).

A form of effectiveness that is later developed, more differentiated, can be set off from the unselfconscious, humbler form in which sounding data are felt merely as stimuli triggering reflexes. For the later-developed form, Kurt Huber's argument claims that any musical listening worthy of the name means, first, experiencing emotional traits objectively, as properties of the music itself, and only secondarily, if at all, transferring them into the listener's own mood. In order to recognize the affective meaning of a piece of music, one need not oneself be stirred.

Ever since antiquity, in esthetic–therapeutic investigations and speculations seeking an explanation for the '*meravigliosi effetti*' of tones, it was the concept of motion that provided a connection between music and affection or ethos. The motions of tones sympathetically release those of the soul, a soul that is often described by the simile of a stringed instrument; both musical and psychic motions are subject to the same laws. The hypothetical 'animal spirits' that were supposed to account for the transfer of physical stimuli into psychic reactions either stretch or contract, either reach out toward some object or withdraw from it. The movements of the animal spirits, according to Nicola Vicentino (1555) and Gioseffo Zarlino (1558), are the reason for the effects of intervals: major 'stretched' intervals of the second, third, and sixth attune to joy, while minor 'contracted' intervals on the contrary attune to sadness. 'What is passionate in us,' wrote Herder concerning the effects of music, 'rises and falls, leaps or creeps, and slowly paces. Now it becomes urgent, now hesitant, now stirred more feebly, now more strongly.'

2.

The eighteenth-century esthetics of imitation, most vigorously and influentially formulated by Charles Batteux in *Les beaux arts réduits à un même principe*, 1773) conceived music's expression of affections as representing, describing passions. A listener assumes the role of relaxed spectator, an observer who deigns to judge the likeness or unlikeness of a depiction. A listener is not himself exposed to the affections that are musically represented, nor does a composer offer up his agitated inner experience in any sounding testimony for which he expects a listener's shared feeling, his 'sympathy.' A composer is more like an artist who paints someone else's emotions than a person who exhibits his own. Thus the composer and theorist Friedrich Wilhelm Marpurg, in his *Historisch–kritische Beyträge zur Aufnahme der Musik* (*Historical–critical contributions to the reception of music*, 1754–62, 1778), demanded:

> In pieces for singing let us seek first to study and determine exactly which affection resides in the words; how high a degree of the affection; from what sort of feelings it is composed... Then let us be concerned to inspect closely the essence of this affection and what sort of motions the soul may be exposed to; how the body may even suffer from it; what sort of motions may be caused in the body... Only then, after having considered, tested, measured, and settled all this exactly, thoroughly, and carefully, then may we entrust ourselves to our genius, our power of imagination and invention.

Music is 'imitation of natural beauty' (*imitation de la belle nature*), just like the other arts that Batteux reduced to the same single principle. 'Animated tones' (*sons animés*) form the model of vocal music, 'inanimate' that of instrumental music. If song is representation of affections, in this view, then how can Batteux imagine instrumental music as intelligible, as anything more than empty sound? Only as 'speaking' or 'painting,' as a weaker reproduction of vocal formulae or as program music. Yet the object of all fine arts, he supposes, is not actual nature as it exhibits itself every day. Utterances of feeling and inanimate noises – the testimony of internal human selves and the acoustical image of an external world – these must be stylized to become capable of standing as objects of art, an art that above all avoids offense to taste. The selective and modifying taste (*goût*) is the esthetic counterpole to nature. Not nature in the raw, but potential 'natural beauty' ('la belle nature, telle, qu'elle peut être') is to be incorporated in art.

Yet, cultivated taste may not necessarily comprehend the beauty that is hidden in nature, the beauty that composers as well as painters or poets should discover and that works of art should exhibit. Against the arrogance of the Enlightened age, Jean Jacques Rousseau proposed, in contrast, his idyllic picture of a prehistoric time in which 'natural beauty' was still present reality. And Rousseau's hypothetical language of primeval ages, the 'original language' whose reconstruction would be the goal of an 'imitation of natural beauty,' had to be both poetic and musical. Herder and Wagner would later agree with Rousseau. Sound, originally, they conceived to be eloquent, and eloquence to be sound. Of the original language only scattered remnants could be extant. The melodic accents and inflections of a voice, in which people of the primeval Utopia expressed their affections, had faded and wilted in modern languages to mere indications. Italian came closer to the original language, thought Rousseau, than French, which was comparatively impoverished in sound. (Gluck's operas, however, forced Rousseau later to revise this judgment.)

3.

The thought that tones might be 'natural signs' of feelings, an idea that governed music esthetics after Dubos, facilitated a transition from the principle of representation to that of expression. Now the theory of imitation, which had assigned composers the role of prudent observers, was rejected as narrow-minded and trivial by Carl Philipp Emanuel Bach, Daniel Schubart, Herder, and Heinse. Now a composer's task was no longer to portray passions, but rather 'to force out his selfhood in music,' as Schubart expressed it in language as drastic as his meaning. Only one who delves into himself and creates out of his inner depths is 'original.' The principle of originality demands not mere novelty but also and above all that a work of art be an 'actual outpouring of the heart.' The old 'painting' of affections has turned into their eruptive testimony. The 'fundamental experience' of the musical storm-and-stress (*Sturm und Drang*), according to Hans Heinrich Eggebrecht, is 'that man can express himself in music.' To echo Schubart again, what has previously been an 'aped feeling' now becomes real.

The esthetics of expression has suffered misunderstanding more than its counterpart, formalism. The saying that music is or should be an 'outpouring from the heart' risks abuse as a justification and alibi of any enthusiastic dilettantism that claims an advantage in its innocence of compositional technique, instead of feeling it as a shortcoming. For this reason, a bit of pedantry may be tolerated in distinguishing various aspects of the principle of expression.

First, a composer's instruction to play a passage 'expressively' (*con espressione*) should not be confused with a marginal note in which he says that the music arose under the duress and dictate of some real feeling. Technical indications for performance can be distinguished from esthetic confessions.

Secondly, any listener who asks about the biographical reality which he supposes entered into a piece of music is behaving extraesthetically, trivially. Musical expression is not to be immediately related to a composer as a real person. Even the extreme 'expressionists' of the eighteenth century, Daniel Schubart and Carl Philipp Emanuel Bach, when they 'expressed themselves through music,' were showing not their empirical person in private life, but their 'intelligible I,' the analogue of a poet's 'lyrical I.' The 'sensibility' (*Empfindsamkeit*), which formed in the century of Enlightenment the complement and reverse side of its strict rationality, was never associated with a lack of taste as the modern term 'sensitivity' can sometimes imply today.

Thirdly, if debaters had more clearly kept in mind the difference between composition and performance, their debate over the esthetic right or wrong of the 'pathological' enjoyment of music, as Eduard Hanslick scornfully called it, might not have been so violent and confusing. The eighteenth-century esthetics of expression – for example, the epigram of C. P. E. Bach that a musician 'could not move others unless he himself was moved' – can be understood primarily, no doubt, as a theory of musical performance. Schubart felt himself a resurrected rhapsode, like a Homeric bard, fallen into an 'inky century,' and it is the rhapsode, not the poet, that Plato refers to in his dialogue *Ion* as having to transport himself into the affections that he wants to arouse. Bach's own performance on the clavichord, as his contemporaries testify, made such a difference in the effectiveness of his sonatas and fantasies that their notation transmitted mere abstract schemes. But, after all, the principle of expression, as an esthetic of interpretation, was acknowledged even by Hanslick, who formulated it as though he were a resurrected Herder or Heinse:

A performer is allowed to liberate whatever emotion sways him at the moment directly through his instrument and to breathe out in his performance the wild storming, the passionate flaming, the cheerful power and joy he is feeling within. The very inner impulse that presses my inward trembling through my fingertips directly onto the string or that agitates the bowstroke or that, in song, actually becomes sound itself, really enables musicians to indulge the most personal outpouring of mood. In this situation, subjectivity emerges as immediately effective sounding in tones, not merely mutely forming in them. (*The beautiful in music, Vom Musikalisch-Schönen*, 1854)

The musical art of expression, if this means composition, script, rather than performance, falls into a paradox. Yet this paradox cannot be disposed of as a flat contradiction, but must be grasped as a living tension, driving historical development onward. If music is striving to become like language, eloquent and expressive – and ever since the late eighteenth century the principle of expression has been indeed the driving force of music history – then it must do two things: on the one hand, in order to make itself understood, music must develop formulae (in opera a whole vocabulary took shape, which overflowed into instrumental music); on the other hand, as 'outpouring of the heart' and expression of someone's own inner being, expressivity demands avoidance of whatever is usual and taken for granted. Under the dominance of the principle of originality, traditionalists could be despised as mere imitators and epigones, though they were irreplaceable for musical culture. The 'model Capellmeister' described by Johann Mattheson in 1739 was still a 'capable composer'; by the nineteenth century 'Kapellmeister-music' became a slur.

Expression, then, is paradoxically yoked to convention, the particular to the general. If expression, being subjective, is unrepeatable, yet at the same time, in order to make itself clear, it yields to a compulsion of becoming established. In the moment when it is realized in any tangible existence, it sacrifices its essence. But, precisely in its dialectic, the principle of expression has become definitive for a historical consciousness and activity in which progressive and conservative traits mutually condition each other. The paradox of the art of expression forces both the production of novelties in steadily accelerating change and the preservation of works from past phases of the development; the paradox forbids what happened in earlier centuries – allowing older works to be discarded and forgotten as obsolete. The fact that musical expression, once achieved, is unrepeatable motivates the tendency to change;

the fact that expression, in order to be understood at all, must be
repeated, supports the maintenance of the past. Progress and historical memory belong together, as two sides of the same thing.

4

Emancipation of instrumental music

Since instrumental music is nothing other than a language of tones, or eloquence in sound, it must always aim its intention at a certain movement of
the heart. To arouse this, it must take due care about the power of intervals, the deft division of movements, the appropriate continuation, and
other things of the sort.

The concept of a 'language of tones' (*Tonsprache*) has become a
cliché. But it must have seemed rather a striking paradox to
eighteenth-century readers who happened on it in *Der vollkommene Capellmeister* (*The model Capellmeister*, 1739, 1782) by
Johann Mattheson, Hamburg's notable composer, writer on music,
and diplomatist. For even as late as the second third of that Enlightened century of *philosophes*, the kind of music that was later called
'absolute' in order to express a sense that it was music proper,
music fully developed, was still not taken seriously; before the
triumphs of the Mannheim orchestra in Paris, even the best-
educated of those who disdained instrumental music dismissed it as
inanimate noise and empty sounding. Rousseau spoke casually of
rubbish (*fatras*) and the question ascribed to Fontenelle and repeated to excess, 'Sonata, what do you want of me?' ('Sonate, que
me veux tu?') implied, with an arrogant gesture, that anything not
immediately clear to a man of common sense (*honnête homme*)
was not worth understanding. Instrumental music, unless provided
by a program-note with some intelligible meaning, was regarded
not as eloquent but simply as having nothing to say.

Hence Mattheson's claim that instrumental music was a
language of tones or eloquence in sound was an apology. The
absence of words needed justifying, although a century and a half
had passed since instrumental music was emancipated from vocal
models, and its significance was recognized by Seth Calvisius,

cantor at St Thomas's in Leipzig, contemporary with Giovanni
Gabrieli and the English virginalists. Calvisius says in his *Melopoiia* (1592, chap. 13) that music has power, even without a text, to
stir passions, because instrumental music, no less than vocal, is a
movement of tones analogous to emotional excitements, defined
and regulated by numbers and proportions.

Etsi autem Harmonia nuda, ut videre est, in instrumentis Musicis, scienter
et perite ab artificibus tractatis, propter numerorum ac proportionum
rationem, quibus sese humanis mentibus insinuat, plurimam in affectibus
excitandis exercet potentiam...

According to Mattheson again, instrumental music differs from
vocal music not in its purpose ('such a pleasure of the hearing as
arouses passions of the soul') but only in its means, which are
fewer, so that it is the more difficult art. Or, it may be, the 'less
complete' (*vollkommen*) art: if there is doubt about the possibility
of making tones a language pure and simple, or of realizing the
'principle of eloquence' in music without any adulterating admix-
ture of meaningless noise, then it must be conceded that instrumental music indeed approaches its goal of becoming eloquence in
sound but never quite reaches it. This is the view of Heinrich Christoph Koch in his *Versuch einer Anleitung zur Composition* (*Essay
of a guide to composition*, 1782–93, vol. II, p. 30). Mattheson
claims, with the pardonable naiveté of first effusion, that a composer must

know how to express truly all the heart's inclinations by means merely of
carefully chosen sounds and their skillful combination without words, so
that a listener can completely grasp and clearly understand the motive,
sense, meaning and force, with all the phrases and sentences pertaining
thereto, as if it were a real speech. Then it is a delight! Much more art and
a stronger power of imagination belong to this achievement without words
than with their help. (p. 208)

It was assumed that a piece of music always exerted the same
effect. If anyone noticed that this assumption did not fit, then the
old doctrine of the four temperaments was invoked to explain exceptions from the rule: whoever failed to recognize cheerful music
as such must be a melancholic type who assimilated into his own
dismal constitution everything he heard. The doctrines of the affections and of the temperaments mutually shielded each other
against disproof by experience.

'Some passages in music were so clear and insistent to him that the tones seemed to him to be words': thus Wackenroder's hero, in *The remarkable musical life of the artist in tones, Joseph Berglinger* (1797).* This fictional composer was transported by music into a 'beautiful poetic frenzy,' into an ecstasy that constituted his real life. (The 'joyous and charming symphonies for full orchestra' that Berglinger 'loved most of all' were presumably works of Haydn.) But the explanation as 'eloquence in sound,' which Wackenroder took over by way of Forkel (1788) from Mattheson, was not the only way of justifying instrumental music and preserving it from condemnation as empty noise. The exponents of the esthetics of imitation in the early and middle eighteenth century, Abbé Dubos and Charles Batteux, who sought to reduce all the arts to one indivisible truth – namely, that art was imitation, *mimesis* – regarded vocal music as imitating speech-intonation, and instrumental music as tone-painting. Even Rousseau in his *Dictionary of music* (1768, p. 225), while he ranked instrumental music rather low, allowed something for 'the musician's genius': 'It paints all pictures by means of sounds.' ('Il peint tous les tableaux par des sons.') As a sort of painting, instrumental music was legitimized: it imitated something, even though in a naive and banal form.

Instrumental music that can be understood neither as language of tones nor as painting, that neither 'speaks' nor 'represents' anything, was regarded as 'mere noise' in Johann Adolf Scheibe's *Critischer Musikus*, 1745. And Johann Joachim Quantz remarks in his *Versuch einer Anweisung, die flûte traversiere zu spielen* (*Essay of a guide to playing the transverse flute*, 1752): 'A continual liveliness or mere difficulty does indeed arouse admiration, but does not especially stir anyone.' Velocity and virtuosity are empty and 'mechanical,' not sensitive and 'poetic,' and therefore they are worthless according to the conceptions of the Enlightened century, which was simultaneously a sentimental one. Two years after Quantz, Johann Adam Hiller speaks, in the first volume of Marpurg's *Historisch–kritische Beyträge*, of 'marvelous, admirable' qualities in wordless music, so that he appears to anticipate Wackenroder's 'spiritual doctrine of today's instrumental music,' but in fact he means the same thing as Quantz: 'leaps, runs, and arpeggios,' the arts of virtuosi like Tartini, which arouse admir-

---

* Wilhelm Heinrich Wackenroder (1773–98) is the only writer of fiction to be treated here at length, Chapter 6. The Berglinger story is part of the young Wackenroder's *Herzensergiessungen eines kunstliebenden Klosterbruders* (*Outpourings of the heart of an art-loving monk*, 1797). Oliver Strunk's translation of the Berglinger story, in *Source readings in music history* (New York, 1950; 1965, vol. V, pp. 10–23), may be familiar to some readers.

ation and amazement but leave the heart empty. The 'marvelous' is the opposite of the 'natural,' the simple musical 'language of feeling.' It is the essence of Baroque superabundance, which has just been left behind as outworn.

But around 1780 'marvels' regained honor in music esthetics. The theory of instrumental music absorbed something from the poetics of Klopstock, which has been characterized, not unjustly, as 'neo-Baroque,' that is, as reacting against the rationalistic esthetics of imitation. True poets and composers have a sense for the sublime and marvelous, beyond mere reason and naturalness, which risk remaining stuck in parsimonious mediocrity. 'The symphony is especially apt for the expression of things grand, solemn, and lofty,' writes Johann Abraham Peter Schulz in Sulzer's *Allgemeine Theorie der schönen Künste* (*General theory of the fine arts*). If listeners are dazzled or even confused – a reproach three decades previously – this now counts toward the glory of a symphony. A symphonic allegro is comparable to a 'Pindaric ode in poetry: it exalts and agitates a listener's soul in the same way and demands the same intelligence, lofty power of imagination, and knowledge of art, in order to succeed.' Artificiality is revered as something sublime. C. P. E. Bach is hailed as 'another Klopstock' in the *Allgemeine musikalische Zeitung* (*General musical news*, 1801),* but a Klopstock who 'used tones instead of words.' Bach 'has demonstrated that pure music is not merely a garment for applied music, nor abstracted from it, but rather ... capable of rising to poetry, which is all the purer the less it is dragged down into the region of vulgar meaning by words (which are always laden with connotations).' The very same absolute music that was 'mechanical' in 1750 now reveals the 'poetic.' The reversal could not be more drastic. And enthusiasm is now so vigorous and generous that it may spill over to lesser composers than Haydn, the inspirer of Wackenroder. Thus symphonies of Cannabich won praise from Daniel Schubart in 1791 with words that anticipate E. T. A. Hoffmann's dithyrambs about Beethoven: 'This is no mere babble of voices ... it is a musical whole whose parts, like spiritual emanations, again form a whole.' The enthusiasts hear in instrumental music an 'esoteric Sanskrit,' an original language of the human

---

* 'Bemerkungen über die Ausbildung der Tonkunst in Deutschland im 18. Jahrhundert' ('Remarks on the development of the art of tones in Germany in the 18th century'), attributed to Triest, ran through eleven issues of the periodical, vol. III. The passages cited are in cols. 300–1. A preceding phrase about C. P. E. Bach deserves notice: 'He was agitated by ineffable *esthetic* ideas, that is, composites of concept and feeling.'

race. What had been an 'admiration' that left the heart empty has become a metaphysical amazement at the 'marvel of the art of tones.'

'You who scorn the music of tones as such and can find no profit in it, then leave it alone without words; stay away from it.' This sentence from Herder's *Kalligone* (1800, vol. II, p. 169) responds, at the distance of a century, to Fontenelle's 'Sonata, what do you want of me?' Herder, having been challenged and stimulated to polemics by Kant's *Critique of judgment*, believes that anyone would have to be deaf or dumb to see in independent music, detached from words and gestures, nothing but empty play. Only in such music, not in vocal music, does emotion attain 'self-perception of itself,' as Hegel expressed it two decades later. Herder exclaims:

What was the something that separated it from everything else, from glance, dance, gesture, and even from the accompanying voice? Devotion. It is devotion that lifts men and assemblies of men above words and gestures, since their emotions then remain nothing – but tones. (vol. II, p. 171)

What Herder called 'devotion' (*Andacht*), the release of feeling from the confinements of prosaic everyday reality, Hans Georg Nägeli in his *Vorlesungen über Musik* (*Lectures on music*, 1826) calls 'mood.' To transport or uplift into a mood that extends beyond the mundane is the essence of instrumental music. It is at the opposite pole from painting tone-pictures or delineating characters and thus from the methods of composition that provided the only justification for despised wordless music discernible to the esthetics of the early and middle eighteenth century. 'The word "character" has been overused in relation to the art of tones – here this always means instrumental music – and invariably this use is an abuse.' (Nägeli, p. 32) Music neither represents nor imitates. It is 'a being at play, nothing more. It has no content, as used to be supposed and despite what anyone might wish to read into it.' But Nägeli's idea of 'play of forms,' though lacking content and conceptions, is not abstract but constitutes a mechanism for evoking indefinite and ineffable feelings. The soul 'hovers, carried along by this play of forms, in the whole immeasurable realm of emotions, now ebbing, now flowing, up and down, plunging with the gently echoing breath of tones to the utmost depths of the heart and then soaring again with the rising impetus of tones to supreme feelings of bliss.' (p. 33) Nägeli's theory of the 'play of forms' has been interpreted as anticipating Hanslick's thesis that 'forms moved by sounding' are the 'content of music,' but Nägeli's theory is more reminiscent of Herder's or Wackenroder's dithyrambs than of the more sober esthetics devoted to what is 'specifically musical,' the esthetics labeled in textbooks 'formalism.'

When Nägeli suggests that wordless music is real music, his suggestion appears in a parenthesis that masks a striking idea as self-evident: '. . . in relation to the art of tones – here this always means instrumental music – . . .' Nägeli's assumption was by no means self-evident in the 1820s. More commonly, in order to avoid having to relinquish familiar esthetics, listeners searched in Beethoven's symphonies for esoteric programs, rather than grasping them as evidence of a transition to the hegemony of instrumental music. (The Pastoral Symphony marks an end rather than a beginning; it has little or nothing in common with nineteenth-century symphonic poems.) If music emancipated from a text was praised as 'independent, granting itself its own existence and shape,' in the *System der Ästhetik* by Hegel's disciple Christian Hermann Weisse (1830, vol. II, p. 54), Weisse was expressing an insight that contradicted accepted opinion, though indeed he was grasping the spirit of his time in concepts, as Hegel proposed. And even Hanslick felt compelled, when he maintained the primacy of instrumental music, to expound his thesis as a polemic.

Nineteenth-century philosophers, laymen in music, approached a professional with mixed feelings of respect for his hard-won knowledge and suspicion that musicians were somewhat limited in culture; the philosophers were often inclined to uphold the prestige of vocal music against the tendencies of contemporary composers. Philosophers distrusted instrumental music, esoteric as well as popular. The exclusive esoteric kind, they thought, 'contributed nothing to the artistic interests of mankind in general,' which Hegel had proposed as matter for formulation by philosophy. The popular kind, in turn, invited a straying into moods and fantasies beyond all boundaries and all good sense. Daydreams aroused the suspicions of an esthetic censor just as they did those of a moralist. And in order to restrain daydreaming, such people praised vocal music with its firm boundaries. 'For a text provides from the start definite conceptions and thereby rescues consciousness from that dreamier element of feeling without concepts in which we may allow ourselves to be led hither and thither without interruption and may preserve our freedom to feel out anything we choose in a piece of music and to feel moved by it in any way we choose.'

(Hegel's *Aesthetics*, ed. Bassenge, vol. II, p. 306). According to Hegel the soul strives naturally and instinctively away from vague and confused things toward limited and clear things. 'From their natural element of indefinite inwardness in some important matter and of subjective immersion in it, our feelings proceed toward concrete observation and more generalized representation of this content.' (vol. II, pp. 269–70)

In Hegel's system, the opinion that instrumental music was incomplete, in need of completion by words, was perhaps a partial aspect of his dialectic, according to which music as art loses what it gains as music while losing as music what it gains as art. But Hegel's opinion congeals to dogma, self-sufficient and proclaimed as such, in the work of Friedrich Theodor Vischer, who was the most important esthetician among Hegelians. 'Mere instrumental music, on the contrary, presents feeling in its purity, i.e., in its unconsciousness; for this very reason it shares the deep deficiency of feeling... All the depths of feeling would never unfold without accompanying consciousness. Only when directed toward definite objects does the whole wealth of the realm of feeling blossom.' (*Ästhetik oder Wissenschaft des Schönen*, 2nd edn, 1923, vol. V, pp. 66–7)

Lack of definiteness looms as a 'defect' of instrumental music in the view of Gervinus, who could support his opinions with the experience of Wagnerian music-drama. (*Händel und Shakespeare: Zur Ästhetik der Tonkunst*, 1868). Gervinus, appealing to eighteenth-century theories of imitation, doubts whether instrumental music has any right to exist. It is 'nothing but imitation of vocal music' (p. 146). It is an abstraction 'capable of presenting no full substance, no plastic life, but only a schema or scheming' (p. 150). And since it is such a pale empty copy of real music – vocal music – it falls on the horns of a dilemma as soon as it claims the character of art. 'Instrumental art at the summit of its development was itself aware that its peculiarity – of lacking content because it did not imitate or refer to any object – was a defect. But its exertions to make up for this lack almost tempt one to call them a tragicomic part of music history' (pp. 159–60). The experiment of program music amounted to no more than 'trying a language that cannot say what it is supposed to say' (p. 164). But on the other hand any instrumental music resigned to being meaningless play hardly deserved the name of art in the emphatic sense. Moreover, to discredit wordless music, Gervinus does not hesitate to type-cast dilettantes as philosophers and professional musicians as technicians. He poses a deceptive antithesis between 'giving form' and the 'intellectual substance' absent from pure instrumental music, between 'laborious craft' and 'esthetic perceptiveness,' between 'technical organization' and 'artistic structure' (p. 152), and between 'marvelous achievements of technique' and 'miraculous works of art' (p. 158). Though Gervinus is a respectable historian, his esthetics degenerates into an apology for dilettantism, the kind of dilettantism that feels all the more securely in possession of the spirit of art the more arrogantly it displays its scorn for technique and lowly craftsmanship.

Thus it becomes easy to understand Arnold Schoenberg's impatience in his *Theory of harmony* (1911), where he speaks of a 'bad esthetics' that he has tried to replace with a 'good theory of craftsmanship.'

5

Judgments of art and of taste

1.

In all fine art the essence consists in form, which lends itself to observation and judgment, wherein our pleasure is simultaneously culture, attuning the mind to ideas... After poetry, insofar as the stimulation and movement of the heart is our concern, I should place ... the art of tones. For although this art perhaps speaks through sheer feelings without concepts, leaving no residue for reflection as poetry does, still it moves the heart more variously and even, though only in passing, more intensely. But of course it is more enjoyment than culture...

Kant's suspicious attitude in his *Critique of judgment* (secs. 52 and 53) toward music's claim to rank among the fine arts is aimed primarily at instrumental music. For Kant as for Rousseau, on whose music esthetics Kant bases his own, instrumental music is liable to the suspicion of being empty sound, devoid of substance. Yet, on the other hand, with his constant care for clear distinctions, Kant sees in wordless instrumental music the real, unalloyed, self-sufficient music. Thus he finds that music is inferior precisely when it is most itself: an agreeable entertainment that does not 'attune

the mind to ideas.' And, correspondingly, as soon as music joins
with a text it loses its own distinctive character but ascends from
pleasure to culture. It is 'fine art (not merely agreeable) only
because it serves as a vehicle for poetry.' (*Anthropology in pragmatic perspective, Anthropologie in pragmatischer Hinsicht,* 1800, sec.
68). To distinguish what is 'fine' or 'beautiful' from what is merely
'agreeable' or 'pleasing' is one of the urgent motives of the *Critique
of judgment*. Having granted to music some 'charm' or 'stimulus'
and 'moving of the heart,' Kant sets these in opposition to 'fine-
ness' or 'beauty.' His opposition is so dogmatic that it becomes
intelligible only when we notice in his expositions, despite their os-
tensibly unhistorical nature and their detachment from immediate
experience, traces of a polemical argument by which a new style is
attempting to equip itself with theoretical foundations. By rigorously separating beauty from agreeableness, Kant justifies classicism, as Rosario Assunto has noticed, in opposition to the rococo
and the sentimental, whose characteristic categories were 'charm'
and the capacity to 'stir.' Kant's abstract deductions are 'ideological,' though not by his conscious intention. His normative propositions, meant to hold universally and unconditionally, are in fact
historically motivated.

   The view that instrumental music is a 'merely agreeable art,'
'more pleasure than culture,' implies that it lacks form, 'the
essence in all fine art,' or that such forms as it has are weak and unsatisfactory. This is a thesis irreconcilable with the opinion commonly accepted among academics that Kant founded 'formalism'
in music esthetics. Indeed, Kant's conception of form is so different
from Eduard Hanslick's that referring to both in the same breath is
misleading, just as, in general, it is a simplistic, unphilosophical
recourse to pigeonhole music-esthetical systems, essays, and aphorisms according to 'trends.' In Kant's view music is a 'play of feelings' (sec. 51) and in his concept of 'feelings' (*Empfindungen*) there
is a fusion of sensuous qualities and emotions, of things that
'charm' and things that 'stir.' Yet Kant also defines beauty in music
as 'form in the play of many feelings' and the form he took for
granted was the 'mathematical form' of tone-relations. 'Upon this
mathematical form alone – mathematical though not represented
by definite concepts – depends the satisfaction that connects mere
reflecting on such a crowd of feelings, simultaneous or consecutive,
with their play, as a universally valid condition of its beauty' (sec.
53). But the 'mathematical form' that could serve as a basis of
music's claim to belong among the fine arts, not merely the agree-

able ones, is a transitory aspect, according to Kant, which vanishes
in the emotional effect. 'Surely mathematics has no part whatso-
ever in the charm and the agitation of the heart produced by music,
but it is rather only an indispensable condition' (sec. 53). Musical
beauty – form – is and remains concealed, while the manifest music
proffers mere pleasure unless it is subordinated to poetry. Kant's
music esthetics may be called dialectical. His thought is reminiscent of Francis Hutcheson's, in *An inquiry into the origin of our
ideas of beauty and virtue* (1726). Both Kant and Hutcheson define
musical beauty formally, as a harmony of representations of tones;
both sharply divide the emotional effect of music from esthetic
judgment, although they do not deny the emotion but even emphasize it.* There is a gulf between art's characteristic dependence on
form and the affective power of music – a power felt more intensely
in the eighteenth century than later, for that age was every bit as
sentimental as it was rational.

It must be admitted that Kant's conception of music's mathematical aspect as its sole form, submerged in its emotional effect, constitutes a drastic limitation. This limitation can be shown in the
light of some assumptions which need not be brought to bear on
Kant's system from the outside as they are implied in the system
itself. Specifically, Kant's music esthetics is open to an immanent
criticism deriving from his conception of time. In the *Critique of
pure reason*, in the chapter on the transcendental esthetic, time has
been defined as a pure form of observation, a general condition for
representing objects. And it would not have been impossible – or
rather, it was an obvious thing to do – to develop from this conception of time an esthetics of music that would do justice to Kant's
purpose of clearly distinguishing beauty from mere agreeableness.
The question of whether an individual feels sound impressions –
isolated, unrelated timbres or chords – as agreeable or disagreeable depends on the individual, so it would be nonsense to wish to
insist that someone else share one's pleasure in the charm of any
particular acoustical event, if the same configuration gives the
other individual pain. But altogether different is the temporal proportioning of simple and complex sensations of tone: this is an
object of universally valid judgment unsupported by concepts; thus
it fulfills the conditions that Kant requires for esthetic judgments
about beauty and ugliness. While the 'mathematical form' of intervals may be only latent, that of rhythms is manifest. Kant's music

---

* Hutcheson speaks of the 'Charm' of 'raising agreeable Passions' (pp. 84–5) in contrast to the 'Harmony of Notes' perceived by a 'good ear' (pp. 27–8).

esthetics suffers from too narrow an idea of the function of time in music. He has conceived this art as merely 'transitory,' always passing away, instead of recognizing that events in time can also be fixed in forms (*Gestalten*).

2.

But if an object is presented as a product of art, to be declared beautiful as such, then ... a basic prerequisite is a conception of what this thing is supposed to be. Now, the perfection of a thing lies in the coordination of its many components with its inner destination to a purpose; hence, the degree of a thing's perfection will have to come into consideration at once in judging artistic beauty, whereas in judging natural beauty, as such, there is no question of purpose ... and teleological judgment serves as basis and condition for esthetic judgment.

Kant's argument here (sec. 48) that judging art presupposes a conception 'of what the thing is supposed to be' appears blatantly to contradict his demonstration (especially in sec. 15, see below) that judgment of taste involves no concepts. One passage revokes what the other maintains, insofar as judgments of art and taste are taken as equivalent.

Section 15, one of the crucial pieces of argument in the *Critique of judgment*, is directed against Alexander Baumgarten, author of *Aesthetica*, 1750. Baumgarten had defined beauty as *perfectio cognitionis sensitivae*, perfection for sensuous perception. Kant's polemic restricts itself to the bounds of an immanent critique. Kant shares Baumgarten's assumption that beauty is judged not according to concepts but rather exclusively on the basis of perceiving, that is, 'esthetically,' in the original sense of the word. Hence, Kant refutes Baumgarten's definition by arguing that anything perfect will necessarily be related to a purpose; measuring its adequacy to the purpose shows its perfection, in other words, the thing is related to a conception of 'what the thing is supposed to be.' Therefore, argues Kant, a definition of beauty as *perfectio cognitionis sensitivae* contradicts itself. To claim that something perfectly fulfills a purpose while its function is unknown would be a paradox. 'In order to imagine in a thing any objective adequacy to its purpose, a prerequisite will be to conceive what sort of thing this thing is supposed to be; and the coordination of the thing's many components with this concept ... is the qualitative perfection of the thing' (sec. 15).

The apparent contradiction between sections 15 and 48 can be resolved only by sharply distinguishing judgments of art from judgments of taste: a judgment of art concerns the formal and technical perfection or imperfection of a structure, while a judgment of taste proclaims an object beautiful or ugly. To judge that a succession of tones is 'perfect' as theme for a fugue or sonata implies not at all that this succession belongs to those melodies that evoke the epithet 'beautiful' or some substitute such as 'the heart's ah! and oh!' Correspondingly, a melody may be felt and judged as beautiful with no need for the listener, who enjoys it and expresses pleasure in it, to entertain any concept of a formal function to be fulfilled by the melody, of its adequacy as a theme. A 'good' theme need not be a 'beautiful' melody, and vice versa.

Works of 'fine art,' 'beautiful art' – that is, works of an art that is fine and beautiful, and works of a sort of beauty that is art – such works are liable to double jeopardy in Kant's system: to the judgment of taste and the judgment of art. 'Teleological judgment [as to perfection] serves esthetic judgment [as to beauty] as its foundation and condition' (sec. 48). Yet only as a prerequisite destined to vanish in its goal and result, like a necessary evil, is this judgment of art accepted. It is a 'suspended aspect,' as Hegel would say. And as Kant himself puts it: 'The purposiveness in a product of fine art, therefore, although of course it is intentional, still must not seem intentional. In other words, fine art must look like nature, although we recognize it as art' (sec. 45). A composer's technique, the trace of his laboring on the work, is to be hidden, so that art appears to have evolved and not to have been constructed. This opinion was appropriated by Wagner, whose efforts to hide his musical technique grew at the same rate as his confidence in it. The conception of 'what a thing is supposed to be,' of the function it fulfills, ought to dissolve into pure contemplation. What is intentional should have the effect of something involuntary. Beauty depends on an appearance of naturalness.

To conceive Kant's esthetics primarily as theory of art would be a misunderstanding. Beauty of nature, not beauty of art, is the phenomenon that motivates the *Critique of judgment*; when categories developed to deal with natural beauty are transferred to works of art, the enterprise cannot succeed without some difficulties. Listening to a fugue 'without concepts' suffers from deficiencies that are not altogether balanced out by a judgment of taste that the piece of music is beautiful. And the argument that we ought to view a work as nature although we know it to be art – this is a paradox which rather expresses the embarrassment into which

Kant has stumbled instead of resolving it. Yet Kant's very inclination to seek beauty primarily in nature and not in art, following
the respected example of Rousseau, was what prevented his subjecting art completely to verdicts of taste and thus of dilettantes,
including even the most informed and cultivated. Kant stayed clear
of the tendency to dissolve art theory into a philosophy of beauty.
This tendency gradually came to the fore in the late eighteenth
century and dominated the nineteenth, but it never distracted Kant
from rigorously distinguishing his concepts. His esthetics preserves
traces of Aristotle's sober idea that art is 'doing' (*facere*), making
works and producing them (sec. 43). No matter that Kant was a
captive of esthetic prejudices of the Enlightened century, nor that
he argued, from philanthropic motives, against the esoteric art of
mannerism and scornfully dismissed works as merely 'mechanical'
if they eluded his conception of beauty, stamped in a classical
mold; no matter that if Bach's fugues had been accessible to him
Kant would doubtless have applied to them the same dismissive
judgment; his decisive testimony is that art need not be beautiful in
order to be art. Anyone who blurs or blots out the distinction
between judgments of taste and judgments of art appeals to Kant in
vain.

3.

Since, therefore, what is beautiful must be judged not by concepts but
rather by the appropriate attuning of imagination to agree with the general
capacity of making concepts – since this is the case, what is to serve as subjective standard for that adequacy to purpose, esthetic but unconditioned,
which is sought in a fine art that would justly claim to being bound to
please everyone? The standard can be no rule nor prescription but rather
only something natural in the subject, something uncontainable in rules or
concepts, that is, a supersensuous substratum, of all the subject's capacities (attainable by no concept of understanding) . . .

In one labyrinthine sentence (sec. 57, remark I, uniting both sentences of the translation) Kant thus summarizes his critique of
taste. The purpose of this critique is to avoid the troubling alterna-
tive between a dogmatism that lays down norms for beauty and a
relativism that takes comfort in the slogan about no disputing over
taste. (The word 'disputing,' insofar as it is meant to be accepted as
a translation of *disputare*, is liable to a misunderstanding, which
distorts a reasonable proposition into a simplistic one. For the
scholastic idea of disputation, to which Kant still adheres, means a

confrontation of arguments confined within the same presuppositions and using the same fundamental concepts, so that in principle
a valid conclusion is possible through debate. The proposition *De
gustibus non est disputandum* signifies not that wrangling is impossible but rather that the wrangle cannot be decided by firm and
rational criteria.)

The 'appropriate attuning of imagination to agree with the
general capacity of making concepts' is nothing other than the 'purposiveness without purpose,' often mentioned but seldom provided with adequate commentary. Here Kant saw one of the
conditions that must be fulfilled by a judgment of taste that would
be 'subjectively universal,' valid for all subjects. If the formula is
not to remain empty, Kant's argument must be followed sympathetically. This argument is as cogent as it is simple. Insofar as there
exists universally valid knowledge founded on concepts, any presuppositions indispensable for this knowledge must be universally
valid too. But among these presuppositions belongs an 'appropriate, purposive attunement' of the senses and power of the imagination. A succession of tones is definable as a figure adequate to
the concept of a fugal theme only if previously it has been perceived
by the 'lower cognitive capacity' as a firmly contoured plastic
melodic form (*Gestalt*) and not as a chaotic agglomeration of tones.
The 'purposive attunement,' however, can be detached from its
purpose, namely, knowledge through concepts. Then it is 'lacking
in concepts' and yet it remains 'universally valid.' Thus it is the
desired way out between the Scylla of dogmatism, judging by reference to petrified concepts, and the Charybdis of relativism, sacrific-
ing the universal validity of judgments of taste. A beautiful thing,
according to Kant, displays itself to the sort of perception in which
senses and imagination function purposively (for the purpose of.
knowledge) but without fulfilling the purpose (formation of a
concept).

If knowledge of objects is communicable, then the mental state must be
universally communicable too, that is, the attunement of the cognitive
powers to knowing in general, and moreover the proportion of those
powers that qualifies a representation (whereby an object is presented to
us) to constitute knowledge, because without this attunement and this proportion as subjective condition of the act of knowing, no knowledge could
arise effectively. (sec. 21)

Kant's 'something natural in the subject but uncontainable in rules
or concepts' is defined on the other hand, in what seems a paradox,

as 'supersensuous substrate,' as a substantial basis of the
subject's 'capacities,' thus of senses, power of imagination, and
reason. Here Kant refers to genius. He means, moreover, following Diderot's distinction, the genius that someone 'has,' not the
genius that anyone 'is.' Kant proclaims that genius is not subject to
any 'rule or prescription.' It is 'purely nature' and, instead of adapting itself to any standard, it becomes the 'subjective standard' for
art, insofar as the art is fine art. 'Genius is the talent – the innate
gift – that provides rules for art' (sec. 46). Moreover, the rules now
provided are rules of beauty, not those of craftsmanship, of making
and producing. Even genius owes the 'mechanical' part of art to
'schooling,' which Kant was far from belittling (sec. 47). To blur his
concept of genius with that of the *Sturm und Drang* would be a
crude misunderstanding.

The idea that there must exist a rule of beauty proceeding from a
subject seems at first outlandish. But this idea loses its appearance
of being unnecessary or even self-contradictory if we recognize and
agree that the collaboration of the cognitive capacities, in which
beauty is constituted, needs a 'proportioning,' an 'attuning' that
amounts to the condition of genius, and that such an attuning is
transmitted from the genius to listeners or viewers. The rule given
to art by genius is nothing other than the principle of regulating the
cognitive capacities – the capacities of knowing.

This attuning is either work or play. Knowledge of objects grows
from work directed toward a goal, namely, the definition of objects
by means of concepts. The impression of beauty grows from mere
play, a to-and-fro among the capacities. The attuning may be undeniable as fact; it is indeed the center around which Kant's thinking
circles in the *Critique of judgment*; but the attuning remains no less
impenetrable to objective knowing. The 'substrate' in which
senses, imagination, and reason are all rooted is 'supersensuous,'
eluding the insight of our understanding, and yet we must assume
that such a substance exists because otherwise the very possibility
of knowing objects would be inconceivable. The attuning is given
by the grace of nature, the nature that is at work in genius and produces, through genius, works of art whose contemplation 'proportions' and balances our capacities. Art is, for Kant, though in a
sense different from Schelling's, an organon of philosophy, a
means of advancing as we grope in the darkness where senses, imagination, and understanding coalesce into knowledge.

6

Genius, enthusiasm, technique

Oh! Did it have to be just his lofty fantasy that destroyed him? – Shall I say that he was born perhaps to enjoy art more than to practice it? – Are those in whom art works quietly, secretly, like a a veiled genius, without disturbing them in their earthly activity, perhaps more fortunately constituted? And yet, does immortal inspiration perhaps demand that anyone who wants to be a true artist must weave his lofty fantasies like a stout strand, bravely and firmly, into this earthly life? – Oh yes, isn't this incomprehensible creative power something altogether different from the power of fantasy? Was it something, as I now imagine, still more marvelous, more divine?

This concludes the report on *The remarkable musical life of the artist in tones Joseph Berglinger*, whose author, Wilhelm Heinrich Wackenroder, dons the mask of an 'art-loving monk.' The monk's reflection grows out of his retrospective survey of an unhappy life. Berglinger became the sacrificial victim of an enthusiasm that consumed itself.

The *furor poeticus*, the 'fine poetic frenzy,' as Wackenroder called it, had been treated with sober irony in Plato's *Ion*, source of all later panegyrics. Socrates demonstrates to Ion, the rhapsode for whom the dialogue is named, that his activity cannot rival an art based on practical knowledge like a physician's or an architect's, but rather is a form of expression to which he is driven by an external power, beyond his consciousness of self. In the state of enthusiasm he is beside himself, a medium and a blind instrument of the god that speaks through him.

Renaissance humanists, such as the music theorists Giovanni Spataro and Pietro Aron, missed Plato's irony, either intentionally or not. They themselves, inspired by philology, felt they were poets or composers. And the 'blessed madness' was celebrated with all the more abandon when the power invoked by poets was a dead god, no longer an object of belief but withered into an allegory, while the 'madness' that this god ordained was more a figure of speech than any psychic reality.

For that very reason, however, the generation of the late eighteenth century, revering Klopstock as prototypical original genius, and having experienced enthusiasm itself, even though this was diluted with sentimentality, inclines to skepticism. Karl Philipp Moritz, Jean Paul Richter, and even Wackenroder are convinced that the idea that flashes upon the poet in his ecstasy must be seized and carried over into a state of sobriety if it is to assume firm and lasting form. A genius content to be 'intoxicated by spiritual nectar' and to go on indefinitely 'dabbling around in the twilit meanders of poetic feelings' will remain sterile, a dilettante and a gusher (*Schwärmer*).

Wackenroder's Joseph Berglinger cuts himself off from the world and yet suffers from being alone. He feels oppressed and rejected equally by the rationalizing of the 'know-it-alls' who can take possession of a thing only by talking about it, and by the provincial impoverishment of the world he has grown up in. He has outgrown his father's pietism but equally he is appalled by the rationalism of the circle that he supposed was the wide world until he became acquainted with it. The 'cultivated people of good taste' in the petty capital are foreign to him, who, having read Rousseau, would like 'to flee into the mountains, to the simple Swiss herdsman.' And just as foreign are the humble souls trapped in everyday reality, 'who find in the traditional expressions of a good heart such an inexhaustible abyss of splendor that their heaven on earth is replete.' Through music Berglinger discovers himself; from music his own inner being seems to sound out to him; music serves him as a means of fleeing people and again he trusts music to guide him back to people. As a composer, Berglinger seeks a 'fellowman' on whom 'heaven has bestowed such sympathy for my soul that he discerns, from my melodies, just what I felt in writing them down and what I wanted so dearly to put into them.' But he sees through himself: 'A fine idea, with which one can deceive oneself quite agreeably for a while.'

It is embitterment against the world, but also bitterness of self-knowledge that Berglinger confesses when he 'pours out his heart' to the monk. Self-pity, a feeling of never being understood because the public is obtuse and unsympathetic, turns into doubt about his own work, into 'downheartedness and uneasy awareness that with all his deep emotion and sincere artistic sense he was useless to the world and far less effective than any craftsman.' If 'deep emotion' is 'put into' a work that keeps it locked up and unrecognized, this emotion is more likely to produce a dilettante than an artist. 'Shall I say,' asks the monk, that Berglinger 'was born perhaps to enjoy art more than to practice it?' There can be no reconciliation between a mechanic who knows his craft but lacks all feeling and a dilettante who loathes the cold, hard world; both are equally justified in their scorn for each other. Complete competence serves, according to Jean-Philippe Rameau in the foreword of his *Treatise on harmony*, 1722, to 'put to work' genius and taste; these without competence would be useless gifts, but with it they can attain esthetic reality in a work: 'Dailleurs cette parfaite connoissance sert à faire mettre en oeuvre le genie & le goût, qui sans elle deviendroient souvent des talens inutils' (Rameau's spelling).

Berglinger has some command of a composer's technique. He is an artist, but one who feels like a dilettante. And he is wrecked by this split. He knows – he expresses it unmistakably in the 'Fantasies on the art of music' that Wackenroder ascribes to him as sketches from the time of his apprenticeship – that what counts is not straying fantasy and violent agitation of the heart, but technique, the 'machine work,' as he calls it with some exaggeration. The system of tones in itself, without emotion 'put in,' is eloquent and express-ive; indeed, according to a theory formulated by Johann Nikolaus Forkel in 1788, the system of tones, as emblem and image of the human soul, was becoming constantly richer and more differentia-ted, as was the soul itself. A mechanically practiced craft breaks out, so to speak, as 'language of feeling.' The essay by Wackenroder–Berglinger on 'The distinctive inner essence of the art of tones, and the spiritual doctrine of today's instrumental music' attempts to explain a resulting surprise:

This is the reason why many pieces, whose tones have been put together by their masters like numbers in a ledger or tesserae for a mosaic, merely according to rule, yet meaningfully and in a lucky moment – when rehearsed by instruments these pieces speak out in splendid poetry, full of feeling, although the master in his expert work may have given little thought to the possibility that the genius bewitched in the kingdom of tones would, for initiated ears, so splendidly beat his wings.

The work produced by composer's skill and luck of the moment then appears to a sensitive listener as emotional expression, as a 'concentration of feelings that would lose their way, in real life.'

Berglinger finds something demonic about mere machinery's sometimes sufficing to touch the heart. He seems to be anticipating the *Tales* of Hoffmann. He sees through music composed 'like numbers in a ledger' and calls it 'machine work,' yet he succumbs to its effect. The 'fine frenzy' into which he is spun as a listener is 'poetic,' not the work itself. And so music seems to him a 'foreign power' of 'flagrant innocence' and 'frightful, oracularly ambiguous obscurity.' The radiance that surrounded music in the young Berglinger's fantasies is transformed into livid twilight.

The enthusiasm, the 'poet's madness' that seizes Berglinger when he composes his last work, is likewise – in a Christian age – more demonic than divine. Berglinger writes his *opus ultimum*, a Passion oratorio, 'in a marvelous inspiration, but always among violent agitations of the heart.' Inspiration is ecstasy, being-beside-oneself, but agitations of the heart pierce one's inner being. Strikingly enough, Wackenroder opposes these two factors as though they contradicted each other and as if the tension between enthusiasm and emotion, between subjection to a 'foreign power' and the self-centeredness of a sensitive person who 'values his inner being above all,' were what is driving Berglinger to destruction.

7

Affection and idea

Music, unlike all other arts, does not represent ideas or phases in the will's objectification, but rather represents the will itself with nothing intervening. This is the basic reason, moreover, why music acts directly on the will, that is, on a listener's emotions, passions, and affections, quickly elevating or even transforming them... Let us now glance at purely instrumental music. For instance, a Beethoven symphony displays the utmost confusion, based nevertheless on the most perfect order; it displays the most violent struggle, which transforms itself in the next moment to the most beautiful concord... But from this symphony all human passions and affections speak at once: joy, sorrow, love, hate, fear, hope, etc., in countless nuances, yet all as if in the abstract without any particularizing: it is their pure form without matter, like a world of spirits without material.

Schopenhauer's metaphysics of music, though lucidly formulated in *The world as will and representation* (vol. II, chap. 39), encounters unexpected resistance from an understanding that concerns itself with the truth-content of what is said. Schopenhauer's proposition that music represents emotions 'in the abstract' and yet 'in countless nuances' seems uncoordinated. A nuanced joy or sorrow is one individually stamped and delineated, thus precisely not that joy or sorrow as such, which according to Schopenhauer forms the subject of music. But 'abstraction' must be understood in context: it does not mean the procedure of organizing a series of phenomena by suppressing deviant traits and fixing common traits into a comprehensive concept, but rather a disregard of the reality and materiality of emotions with no loss of their individual definiteness. Affections and passions depicted in music, accordingly, are abstract-individual, 'a world of spirits without material,' but with firmly outlined forms. 'But [music's] generality is by no means that empty generality of abstraction, but quite a different sort, and it is bound up with continual clear definiteness.' (vol. I, sec. 52)

Schopenhauer's doctrine that music is 'by no means, like the other arts, an image of ideas, but rather an image of the will itself' (vol. I, sec. 52) has sometimes been naively supposed to exalt music into the infinite. To be sure, this dogma does ascribe to music a metaphysical dignity, but this dignity has a thoroughly equivocal character: proximity to the real essence behind phenomena, to the *ens realissimum*, means entanglement rather than uplift. For although Schopenhauer often appeals to Plato, he departs radically from the tradition of metaphysics by painting the thing-in-itself in dark colors instead of bright. The essence of things, as it comes into the view of detached philosophical observation, is not the idea of goodness, of right order, that holds Plato's thinking in orbit, but rather a blind tangled will and urge, exhausting itself in alternation between the unrest and pain of want and the boredom of achieved peace. The supreme degree of reality, according to Schopenhauer, in blatant contradiction to Plato, is the lowest degree of perfection. And the basest senses are those which most clearly manifest the will, the thing-in-itself.

Tones can directly arouse pain and they can also give pleasure directly by way of the senses, without reference to harmony or melody. The sense of touch is still more subject to this direct influence on the will, since touch is one with the whole body's feeling; yet there is still a kind of touch without either pain or pleasure. But smells are always agreeable or disagreeable; tastes even more so. The last two senses therefore are the most deeply implicated with the will; hence they are always the most ignoble. (vol. I, sec. 38)

The fact that music 'acts directly on the will, that is, a listener's emotions, passions, and affections' is more a disgrace than an excellence. Without Schopenhauer's having made this explicit, it is only consistent with his metaphysics.

A listener, to avoid the baser effects of music, must disconnect it from himself and regard it at a distance, instead of personally undergoing the emotions transmitted by it. The affections represented in music, as images of the will, are to be considered analogous to the (Platonic) Ideas, or, in terms of scholastic philosophy, the universals prior to the thing (*universalia ante rem*). 'Concepts are the *universalia post rem*, but music presents the *universalia ante rem*, and reality the *universalia in re*' (vol. I, sec. 52). Ideas are separated from concepts by a chasm. Concepts are mere instruments in a world of purposes, a world subject to the tyranny of blind tangled will; Ideas, on the contrary, come into the view of a 'disinterested' contemplation, which submerges itself in a thing for its own sake, instead of pursuing a goal. 'Only in the state of pure knowing, where a man's will and its purposes together with his individuality are entirely removed from him, can there arise that pure objective intuitive perception in which the (Platonic) Ideas of things are apprehended' (*Parerga and paralipomena*, vol. II, sec. 206). Ideas – *universalia ante rem* – are, on the lowest level, impressions like those of weight or rigidity.

Every quality of matter is always appearance of an idea, and as such capable also of esthetic contemplation, that is, knowledge of the idea represented in the matter. This, now, is valid even for the most general qualities of matter, without which it does not exist; the ideas of such qualities are the weakest objects of will. Such are weight, cohesion, rigidity, fluidity, reaction to light, etc. (*The world as will and representation*, vol. I, sec. 43)

Weight and rigidity, concepts in everyday usage, are ideas in esthetic contemplation. The distinction between concepts and ideas is correlated with the difference between a perception directed to purposes and a perception that forgets self in contemplation. Yet Schopenhauer's thought is not to be grasped directly and easily. One might ask what distinguishes the esthetic impression of weight or the weighty impression transmitted by a thing from the weight measured or valued in everyday commerce with things.

The esthetic impression of weight – in which Schopenhauer says that the 'Platonic Idea' is shown, and which guarantees its reality – refers to an object from which the impression arises; something impresses. But at the same time weight itself is contained in the impression, so that it is possible to speak meaningfully of a 'weighty impression' instead of an 'impression of weight.' The quality that Schopenhauer calls Idea adheres to the thing as well as the impression. (Josef König, *Sein und Denken, Being and thinking*, 1937, sec. 4.)

The duality becomes more comprehensible if the weight regarded as idea is relieved of predicates that concern exclusively one or other of the two aspects, either the object or its effect. To be green is a trait of a thing; to say that a tree made a green impression would be nonsense. And the same is true of the concept of weight in everyday usage. A predicate like 'clear' (*deutlich*), on the contrary, characterizes only the effect. If one regards an impression of weight as similarly clear, then 'clear' is a quality of the impression itself, not of the object that evokes it. A blurred impression can gradually become a clear one, without need for the object contemplated to change. The ideas that Schopenhauer means, accordingly, waver in a middle range between a predicate for the thing and one for its effect. On the other hand, it is true that the idea of weight, if it is to be grasped as Platonic, is not abstracted from experiences with weighty objects, as a concept is abstracted from experiences, but rather the idea is as if contributed by the beholder, even though unconsciously, and then is simply recognized in the reality. 'Green' is a designation for a quality encountered by beholders in reality. But an impression of weight is an idea, which beholders attach to an object that is not so much a vehicle of the idea as a pretext for its appearance. The fact that someone has often in the past handled weighty objects does not preclude his having now, for the first time, an impression of weight, in a moment of esthetic contemplation, nor his believing that only now he recognizes what weight is in general.

In the context of Schopenhauer's system, his philosophy of art can be seen as an attempt to 'rescue' Platonism, the phantasmagoria of a 'world behind the world' ('backworld,' *Hinterwelt*, to use Nietzsche's word for it); on a route (or detour) to this rescue he encounters esthetics. The moments of self-forgetting esthetic contemplation, released and redeemed from the everyday, are to guarantee that our conviction of the existence of ideas is no madness. The burden of having to serve as an 'organon of philosophy' is settled on art.

The difference between concepts and ideas, Schopenhauer believes, must become manifest in the difference between the experiences whereby they become accessible or comprehensible. But no matter how undeniably esthetic contemplation, in which impressions like those of weight or rigidity assume the lucidity of ideas, may be a different form of experience from the everyday perception that uses instrumental concepts oriented toward purposes, still a skeptical question is readily posed: whether the 'pure recognition' of the idea of weight may not be founded, contrary to Schopenhauer's dogma, on commerce with weighty objects. What is displayed to esthetic contemplation is something ultimate, derived, rather than something primordial, fundamental; rather superstructure than substructure. The claim that it is original and immediate, not possible to trace from previously achieved formations of abstract concepts, is questionable. One can hardly repress a suspicion that the ideas whose survival Schopenhauer would like to insure through esthetics are nothing other than concepts, transfigured, shining in the light of devotional contemplation. The 'work of the concept' (Hegel) is laid aside, so to speak. The mind's spontaneity, its category-forming activity, which Kant discovered through the objects of consciousness that appear to be data from the external world, freezes in the gaze of esthetics to a mere correlation, a static condition in which 'idea' and 'pure recognition,' according to Schopenhauer's formulation, are fitted to each other. But this esthetic 'rescue' of ideas is precarious and threatened: the realm of esthetics is a realm of appearance and even ideas sink to this realm if they are entrusted entirely to esthetic contemplation.

8

Dialectics of 'sounding inwardness'

A musician does not abstract content from each and every thing [like a sculptor], but rather finds content in a text that he sets to music, or else, more independently, clothes some mood for himself in the form of a musical theme, which he proceeds to work out further. But the real field of his composition remains a more formal inwardness, pure sounding. And his penetration into the content proceeds not as an outward constructing, but rather as a retiring into the inner life's own freedom. It is a voyaging of the composer within himself. In many kinds of music it is even a process of testing and confirming that as artist he is free from the content.

Hegel's sentence (in German all the above is a single sentence) defines a boundary between music and sculpture, which 'constructs outward.' In this sentence from his *Lectures on esthetics* (vol. II, p. 266) Hegel formulates a dilemma that is inescapable for music, 'sounding inwardness.' While music's 'real field' is unconstricted 'pure sounding,' its emancipation from a content, whose meaning for inner being music expresses in tones, leads to exhaustion and sterility. Hegel never tires of putting down absolute music, music detached from every content, as 'empty, meaningless.'

Especially in recent times has music thus retired into its own element, cut loose from any import that was previously clear in itself. And all the more, for this reason, has music lost power over the whole inner being, since all the enjoyment it can now offer relates only to one side of art – namely, to a mere interest in purely musical features of composition and its skill, a side of art that is an affair only of connoisseurs, less appealing to the artistic interests of mankind in general. (p. 269)

Here a reminder of Hegel's challenging proposition about the end of art comes to the surface. 'The spirit of our world today,' which has attained self-awareness in Hegel himself, is now, as a philo-sophical spirit, 'rising above the level on which art offers the best way of becoming aware of the Absolute.' Art is losing 'substantial interest.' Granted, the fate of being left behind by 'the spirit' does not prevent further progress in art's technique, in 'purely musical features' in the case of music. Yet Hegel dismisses the 'side of art that is an affair only of connoisseurs' with a gesture of contempt. It is music's hard luck that it forfeits something essential in substance at the very moment when it arrives at its maturity as 'pure sound-ing.' A composer's 'retiring into inner being's own freedom' risks becoming a step into emptiness and abstraction. What music wins as music it loses as an art 'appealing to the artistic interests of mankind in general.'

'The principle of music is constituted by subjective inwardness' (p. 230). This is the 'element' in which music moves. Yet it would be mistaken to count Hegel as a partisan of any esthetics of emotion. He was suspicious of such dreams as those in which Wack-enroder's Joseph Berglinger lost himself when listening to music. Hegel's reflections proceed and catch fire neither from music's working on affections nor from emotions that a composer expresses and preserves in tones. Rather, for him, inwardness is a 'field,' analogous to the 'outwardness' of space: in the latter medium, spirit realizes itself in the forms of architecture and sculp-ture; in the 'field of inwardness' there appears 'substantial import,' and inwardness is a 'way in which it comes to life.'

Hegel defines spirit as content and content as spirit.

Only if, in the sensuous medium of tones and their manifold figuration, something spiritual is expressed in a fitting way, can music too ascend to

true art, regardless of whether this content achieves its more exact designation through words or must be felt less definitely from the tones and
their harmonic relationships and melodic animation (pp. 271–2).

The crucial difference is not that between vocal and instrumental
music, although Hegel's interest applies primarily to vocal, but
rather that between the appearance of an import or content and the
lack of it. Such an import or content is a substance that even a text
may not exhaustively express but only indicate, so that room is left
for music.

The way in which music submerges itself in a content may be
either objective, directed toward some thing, or subjective, directed inward. Either, 'in a Crucifixus, for example,' music grasps
(within the limits drawn for it by its medium) 'the deep implications
in the concept of Christ's passion, as his divine suffering, death,
and burial,' or else music expresses 'a subjective feeling of being
stirred, of sympathy or individual human sorrow about this occurrence' (p. 304). While in a setting of the ordinary of the mass, or a
Biblical text, it may more likely be the 'substantial inner depth of a
content as such' that music tries to attain, elsewhere, in reflective
arias on free poetic texts, music represents 'the life and activity of
an import in some single subjective inner being' (p. 272). But never
does music evade its medium, inwardness, no matter whether
objective or subjective expression as its concern. Always, music is
confined to 'making inwardness comprehensible for the inner
being' (p. 272), be it the inwardness of a meaning contained in a
content – 'a Crucifixus, for example' – or the inwardness of subjective emotion. And yet inwardness, the 'field' of music, is a far-flung
concept in Hegel's philosophy. Within this field fall not only the
feelings evoked by a content but also the very 'inner meaning of a
thing' insofar as it is accessible to emotion.

A music that incorporates spiritual content, a music that
expresses either the interior aspect of an object or inner movements of feeling, rises above the thing it is embracing at the same
time. Music 'transforms the inner being's rapture into a perception
of rapture, into a free lingering with it, and thereby liberates the
heart from the pressure of joys and sorrows' (pp. 298–9). Here
Hegel lyrically celebrates 'the free sounding of the soul.' But as a
judge he is merciless, condemning even the highest form attainable
to music because it represents only one aspect of music's spiritual
content in a version that is now left behind by the progress of
History delineated in Hegel's system. His thesis that 'truly ideal

music' – he names Palestrina, Durante, Lotti, Pergolesi, Gluck, Haydn, and Mozart, but not Beethoven – is 'free in jubilant delight as well as in supreme sorrow, and blessed in its outpouring' (p. 306) is followed by the plunge to his antithesis: the 'sounding play of self-perception,' celebrated as a 'liberation,' risks becoming 'general and abstract' and finally even 'empty and trivial' (p. 309).

Hegel's philosophy of music is stamped, in every phase of its development, with his apprehension that emancipating music, and emancipating a soul that retires into itself in 'pure sounding,' will lead off into sterility.

It may be tempting to try to explain the dialectics to which Hegel subjects music as simply necessitated by his system, so as to get rid of the unassimilable transformation from enthusiasm to reproach. But such an attempt would be futile. Undoubtedly, there is a further thought behind the claim that 'the spiritual inner being' does not persist in 'pure sounding' but proceeds 'from mere concentration of the heart to observations and ideas and their forms constructed by means of fantasy' (p. 264): namely, that music, as art of 'non-objective inwardness,' is a step on the way to poetry, just as music has proceeded, in its turn, from the decomposition of sculpture and painting. But Hegel's system scarcely represents an explanation; rather the system itself needs establishment and justification. By Hegel's own criteria, a system is abstract and arbitrary, forced on objects from outside rather than developed from within them, unless it results from the inner motion of the actual state of affairs. A question would be in order about the factual accuracy of Hegel's thesis, not merely about its place in his system: is it true, as he asserts, that 'sounding inwardness' has a tendency to 'cut loose from content' and that it meets the misfortune that a moment of transition – a peak moment between restraint and freedom –. cannot be held fast but rather threatens to topple into meaninglessness? Again, to claim that Hegel's prognosis for music has been disproved by subsequent history would be exaggerating. 'Art's cultural function,' as it is called by Helmut Kühn, has indeed weakened.

The dialectics of 'sounding inwardness' changed, after the 'fall of Hegelianism,' into a restrained philosophy of music, that of Friedrich Theodor Vischer in his *Ästhetik oder Wissenschaft des Schönen*, 1840–57. Vischer still handed down the heritage of Hegel's thinking, to be sure, but in a form blunted by 'common sense.' The leading argument of his philosophy of music is a proposition, more psychological than metaphysical, that music is 'sounding emotion,' the 'indivisible whole of tone and emotion' (2nd edn, 1923, vol. V, p. 19). This formula, however, is a paradox, though not obviously so. Vischer himself despaired of resolving it in a way that would be scientifically acceptable. Without expressing explicit uneasiness, he was disturbed, not to say dismayed, by Eduard Hanslick (Hanslick's *The beautiful in music* is the focus of chap. 9, below. See also le Huray and Day), who argued that the searching for motivations of the forms of musical works in emotions adhering to them, or hidden in them, was fruitless. For forms, according to Hanslick, are always precise, firmly bounded, and concrete, whereas emotions remain vague, indefinite, and abstract if they lack concepts and objects, yet such vague emotions are the only ones accessible to music. And from hazy generality nothing distinctly individual can be derived.

It would be a crude misunderstanding to think that those estheticians who have been labelled formalists would deny the existence of emotional traits in music. Hanslick acknowledges that motions of melody and harmony are analogous to the 'dynamics' of emotions. Feelings are characterized by tension and resolution, forms of process that resemble those of music. To borrow the words of a modern Gestalt-psychologist, Wolfgang Köhler, 'Quite generally, both emotional and intellectual processes have characteristics which we also know from music, i.e., from auditory experience. *Crescendo* and *diminuendo, accelerando* and *ritardando*, are obvious examples' (*Gestalt psychology*, 1929, p. 248, 1947 edn, p. 230).

The problem was not the existence or non-existence of emotional traits in music, but their definiteness or indefiniteness; around this problem turned the dispute between formalists and their opponents. Vischer conceived the problem in the way it was formulated by Hanslick. He reproached older esthetics of emotion for having been so blind as not to see the difficulty or so negligent as to pass it by. The older esthetics, he thought, 'summarily represented inner being as emotion and could not discover in the simple fog of emotion those lines of demarcation that constitute the original basis of all the distinctions in which moves the formal life of the art of tones' (p. 25). This judgment is too sweeping to be fair. A line of thought stretches back into the eighteenth century proposing that analysis of works of art may facilitate psychological discoveries and insight into individual emotional processes, and thus that esthetics may be, so to speak, an instrument of anthropology, a tool that serves people's interest in their own human nature. The proposal, however, was not so much followed up as repeatedly proclaimed. While the principle was set forth with emphasis, the fact remains that in music esthetics analyses of particular works are rare.

Vischer makes various attempts to define 'sounding emotion' and their diversity betrays how painfully clear the difficulty must have seemed to him. In order to meet Hanslick's objection, he tries to define 'sounding emotion' as an individual thing. He describes it as a fleeting, inapprehensible awareness: 'The individual [emotion] will find its expression in music, therefore, but only as something nearly apprehended, which vanishes into the dark again as too indistinct, the moment anyone wishes to grasp it' (p. 69). Vischer formulates as a paradox the embarrassment to which his principle exposes him. But he ascribes the 'amphibolic character' to the thing itself – emotion – and not to his cognitive method: 'Emotion . . . is without distinctions yet rich in inner distinctions; it is without an object yet allows its object to be apprehended' (p. 62). Music 'is the richest art: it expresses inmost things, utters the unutterable; yet it is the poorest art, says nothing' (p. 64).

Vischer confesses that the esthetics of emotion is forced to beg the question (*petitio principii*). Yet he proclaims this defect as dauntlessness: 'We have dared so far to face the reproach of arguing in a circle, of making deductions from a principle that should have been deduced, in order only then to deduce the latter from the former, inasmuch as our speculations about what underlies music's world of forms in the interior of emotion are gained from the very speculation to which we then proceed as a consequence' (p. 42). Is this circle legitimately hermeneutic? Only analyses of particular works could show, and these are lacking with Vischer. Finally he implicitly abandons even his leading thesis that emotion is the foundation of form. 'Before emotion is worked out,' he admits that 'as material' it is always 'relatively crude and formless,' afflicted with 'all deficiencies and accidents' (p. 51). Thus the emotion that underlies form is not individual, but rather what is individual is only the Gestalt that emotion assumes through form. To be sure, an individual character already inheres, foreshadowed, in the 'emotion as material,' according to Vischer, but this individuality is realized only in form. Moreover, in the same moment when emotion acquires sounding existence it ceases to be emotion; individual emotion exists only as a passing factor in a transition from 'emotion as material,' which is still 'crude,' to the Gestalt of tones in which the emotion expires, 'vanishes into the dark.'

9

The quarrel over formalism

If a question arises as to what is to be expressed with this tonal material, the answer is: musical ideas. A musical idea, completely demonstrated, needs nothing more to be beautiful; it is its own purpose and not at all merely further means and material for representing emotions and thoughts; yet at the same time music can possess that symbolic significance, mirroring grand cosmic laws, which we find in everything artistically beautiful, and in just as high a degree. Forms moved in sounding are the sole and single content and object of music.

Eduard Hanslick's declaration about 'forms moved in sounding' (*tönend bewegte Formen*) is often quoted and nearly as often misunderstood. It is the center around which he groups the aphorisms and digressions composing his treatise *The beautiful in music* (*Vom Musikalisch-Schönen*, p. 32). He intended his slogan as a challenge to the esthetics of emotion, which he called 'putrified' (p. 5). His argument was formulated, not without reason, as a paradox, a *quid pro quo* of opposing concepts: form is declared to be content, thus its own opposite. This provocative claim unleashed a quarrel, a controversy that seems not yet to have come to a conclusion. If Hanslick's claim has been worn down into the trivial statement that music is nothing but form and that form is an empty, expressionless sounding, this should not be blamed on Hanslick. He did use unfortunate metaphors – 'arabesque' and 'kaleidoscope' – when he was stirred up to polemics, but on the other hand he stated unmistakably that what he understood by form was inner form, the *energeia* identified in the philology of Wilhelm von Humboldt and especially of Jacob Grimm, whose authority Hanslick invoked: 'Forms constructed from tones are ... intellectual spirit taking its outward form from within' ('sich von innen heraus gestaltender Geist,' p. 34). Hanslick claims, if he is taken literally, not only that form is spirit's expression, spirit's form of utterance, but that form itself is spirit. In his esthetics, 'form' is an analogue of 'musical idea' and he defines the term 'idea,' depending directly on Vischer and indirectly on Hegel, as a 'concept purely and completely present in its reality' (p. 16). Thus, a form, not less than a musical idea, is an essence that is 'completely demonstrated,' and correspondingly, form is not merely the appearance of some essence that should be sought outside music, in emotions and programs. Since Hanslick conceives form as spirit and essence, he can say meaningfully and consistently that form is a 'content' appearing in the material of tones, or realized therein.

The extremely distinctive place occupied in music by its import in relation to the categories of form and content now becomes clear. An emotion that flows through a piece of music is customarily viewed as the piece's content, its idea, or its spiritual import, while the specific forms of the tones, artistically created, are viewed on the contrary as mere form, image, sensuous garment of that supersensuous thing. But precisely the specifically musical part is a creation of an artistic spirit, with which a perceptive spirit unites in understanding. (p. 72)

Music is 'language' and composing is a 'working of spirit in material fit for spirit' (p. 35).

The idea of founding the concept of musical form on the concept of spirit in musical language saves esthetics from fumbling around in the 'general fog' (Vischer) of the esthetics of emotion. But on the other hand this idea tends to dissolve esthetics into history; the spirit of language (or musical language) is historical. Hanslick drew back from this consequence. He even accused Hegel of having 'insensibly confounded his predominantly art-historical viewpoint with a purely esthetic one' (p. 46), as if he could dispose of Hegel's exertions to combine system and history with a rather impertinent appeal to the expertise of disciplines strictly separated from each other. Hanslick's polemic against the esthetics of emotions is based on something 'purely esthetic.' His crucial argument in this polemic is the proposition that 'the effect of music on emotion' – which thus is not denied – possesses 'neither the necessity, nor the continuity, nor at last the exclusivity that must be demonstrated by a phenomenon in order to establish an esthetic principle' (p. 9). But this argument is weak on two counts: First, orientation toward the exact natural sciences is dubious – in esthetics it leads to ruin probably more often than the loose speculation it decries – and second, despite all Hanslick's scruples about the 'necessity' and 'continuity' of his principles, he cannot avoid admitting that not only the emotional import of music is perishable, but that even a form conceived as spirit, that is, 'the beautiful in music,' is mortal. 'There is no art that uses up so many forms so soon as music... Many compositions that far surpass the everyday level of their time can be

described without injustice as "pieces that were beautiful once"'
(p. 41). The 'continuity' that Hanslick misses in the esthetics of
emotion is lacking in his own 'esthetic principle' as well. The idea of
a timeless esthetic, which he hankered after, is a will-o'-the-wisp.
When he argues that beauty is complete in itself, that a musical
work of art represents 'a specific esthetic structure not conditioned
by our feeling,' and that this structure must be 'comprehended by
scientific observation, set free from any psychological subsidiaries
relating to its origin and its effect' (p. 52), Hanslick's argument is
merely the expression of an epoch – the classicistic epoch – no less
than the old esthetics of emotion proposed by Daniel Schubart or
Carl Philipp Emanuel Bach, against which Hanslick aims his argument.

Although Hanslick endeavored to define conditions of 'the
beautiful in music' that would be universal, detached from history,
he was driven against his will to historicize his esthetic categories.
But this by no means diminishes the significance of his idea that
form in music should be understood as inner form, as 'spirit taking
outward form from within.' This idea was not grasped, or else it
was evaded, by Hanslick's opponents, mired in an insidious habit
of treating form and content as opposites. (Fastening on the comparison of music with an arabesque – a comparison that Hanslick
himself withdrew a few pages later – was a petty trick in the polemics against 'formalism.') Without assuming, as Hanslick did,
that form was no mere outward appearance but rather an essence,
'musical idea,' it would have been nonsense to declare that form
was the 'content' of music, nonsense to turn over to form the function assigned to affect or mood in the rival esthetics of emotion.
But, while a resolution can be found for the paradox Hanslick used
to stir up the prevailing esthetics, still no one should overlook the
fact that any author's true meaning, if it remains hidden and never
understood, signifies less in history than a misunderstanding that
forges its way into history.

Some 'inner form' of music had been spoken of decades earlier,
in Friedrich Rochlitz's justification for J. S. Bach's musical esoteri-
cism: 'Tight-fisted thrift and tenacious though far-reaching
economy with material must look beggarly, scrawny, monotonous,
and dried-up to people incapable of following inner form, who
want to be fascinated by magnificence and manifold outer forms.'
The inner form Rochlitz means is spirit, but it is inseparable from a
composer's technique.

As Hanslick, too, was convinced, nothing would be more false than to see an either/or choice in the distinction or opposition between form and expression. This opposition underlies many descriptions of ways of listening and types of musical works. If it were a matter of alternatives, it would mean that one choice excluded or repressed the other. But obviously there are no musical impressions without some tinge of emotion; if there were, they would be borderline cases with no relevance for esthetics. This can be demonstrated by experiments, as shown especially by Felix Krueger,* founder of wholistic psychology. Even the feeling of emptiness evoked by some études, an emptiness that seems to belong to the pieces themselves as a trait, is undeniably an emotion. Therefore the notion of a music without expression is wretchedly abstract, an idea with application to reality. And likewise the opposite extreme, a music that stimulates emotional excitement without awakening attention as a sounding object fit for esthetic perception, doubtless constitutes an item of everyday reality but it is a fact outside the range of esthetics.

Psychological facts, then, were less at issue than philosophic–esthetic norms and criteria in the controversy between estheticians of form and those of emotion or expression. An adherent of the 'putrified esthetics of emotion' stood accused of enjoying his own condition, the mood he was put in by music, rather than apprehending the esthetic object, the musical work and the spirit it expressed. A formalist, in turn, who scornfully dismissed as extra-esthetic all emotions evoked by music, though not denying them, was found guilty by his opponents not so much of scientific error as of moral turpitude. Sober insistence on seeking the beautiful in music nowhere except in the notes seemed a betrayal of the enthusiasm that music aroused and should arouse, regardless of what its content might be.

The esthetics labeled 'formalism' might better be characterized as esthetics of 'the specifically musical' if we mean to do it justice. (The label was pasted on by opponents of this esthetics, alarmed that 'formalists' would reduce music to an empty meaningless game.) What Hanslick finds more essential than the idea of beauty – reigning over all arts universally and uniformly – is material 'fit for spirit,' not inert matter; through this material one art is dis-

* Felix Emil Krueger (1874–1948), philosopher and experimental psychologist, may become known to some readers for the first time here, as he has to the translator. His connections with music, England, Brazil, and the USA, as well as the strength and distinction of his ideas on value and wholeness, make him more appealing than Dahlhaus takes time to indicate, though these ideas seem to pervade Dahlhaus's thinking. See Krueger's listing in the bibliography.

tinguished from another; which kinds of import the several arts are able to express depends on their material. Robert Schumann believed that 'the esthetics of any one art is that of the others; only their material is different.' And August Wilhelm Ambros declared even in 1856, two years after the publication of Hanslick's treatise, that a conviction of the unity of art was widely accepted: 'Today, fortunately, everybody has learned to recognize that the single arts are only prismatic refractions of one and the same beam of light' (*The boundaries of music and poetry, Die Grenzen der Musik und Poesie*, 1872, p. viii). Like Schumann before him, Ambros gave the name 'poetry' to the aspect that distinguishes a work of art from a merely mechanical structure, in music no less than in painting.

From the beginning we want to remember that poetry forms the life-breath of all arts, their transfiguring ideal motive, and that this poetry ultimately comes to us as an independent art on its own, somewhat as philosophy not only constitutes the foundation of all individual sciences but also appears as a scientific field with its own boundaries. (pp. 12–13)

Hanslick differed. Able to support his view with an observation of Grillparzer, he appealed to the principle of autonomy against the esthetics of music-as-poetry, in which he recognized a danger of putting music at the mercy of poetry. He insisted that music was 'absolute' and could exist in its own right. We may readily understand his suspicious attitude toward subordinating music to literature – a subordination of course not intended by the concept of the 'poetic,' but incited when the concept was crudely misinterpreted. Yet on the other hand Hanslick's principle of the 'specifically musical,' his basic proposition that the traits distinguishing one art from another are the essential ones, is undeniably a prejudice. Any depth-psychologist might suspect that this prejudice arises from some need for firmly distinct competencies rather than from insight into the state of affairs.

　　Hanslick's giving the title of 'content' to 'forms moved in sounding' attests not only that they are spirit but also that they fulfill a function that was ascribed to the 'content' of music by the esthetics of emotion, which defined the content as affect: the function served is that of theme. Since forms are taking over the role of affects, they take along the designation 'content.' The opinion Hanslick argues against is expressed in embryo by Johann Jacob Engel, cited by Hanslick (p. 10): 'A symphony, a sonata, etc., must contain the exposition of one passion, which, however, yields many feelings.' The theme to be 'exposed' or 'expounded,' the 'charge' of a musical work – what holds together its component parts – is an affect, according to Engel. Hanslick declares, arguing against Engel, that the theme of a movement is the tone-structure exposed at the beginning, not the emotion expressed in it. This tone-structure is the center around which all details of a work gather and to which they are all connected.

The 'form' of a symphony, overture, or sonata is the name for the architectonics of connected details and groups of which the piece consists. More precisely, then, form is the symmetry of these parts in their succession, contrast, return, and development. The themes elaborated in such architectonics are accordingly grasped as content. (pp. 100–1)

The themes, called 'content' by Hanslick as well as Engel, are not provided to music from outside, as affects or as a program; rather the themes themselves are music.

10

Program music

Furthermore, it is the unity of the poetic–musical, and the progress to a new consciousness of this unity, that deserves to be called the essential novelty in the artistic creations under discussion [Liszt's symphonic poems]. In earlier phases, but especially with Beethoven, the conscious thought – the preponderance of poetic idea – emerges only along with a soaring of ideals and a gravity of contents, as the end result; but here [with Liszt] these factors constitute a point of departure, a foundation of the whole creation. Hence, this conscious side now has a commanding significance. In Liszt's works we see that earlier process concluded; the summit of thinking, toward which everything strives, has been achieved with precision, and thereby the preponderance of idea has been elevated to governing principle.

The defense of program music in Karl Franz Brendel's challenging thesis that the symphonic poem is the outcome and higher stage of the symphony, set forth in his *Geschichte der Musik,* 4th edn, 1867, p. 643, depends on Hegel's esthetics, with its scheme of a philosophy of history. According to Hegel, the historical development of the arts represents a system in which music appears as a stage on the way to poetry: in music's very essence, which Hegel defines in terms of philosophy of history, there dwells a drive to go beyond

itself. Music cannot persist within itself, in that 'abstract inwardness' where it shrinks back as 'pure sounding.' Music tends to be
dissolved into the 'unity of the poetic–musical,' as Brendel calls it.
Hegel explains, in his *Aesthetics:*

> Our feelings, moreover, proceed from their element of indefinite inward
> immersion in some substance and of subjective involvement with it, on
> beyond to a more concrete observation and a more general idea of this
> content. Even in a musical work this can happen, as soon as the feelings it
> arouses in us, according to its own nature and artistic animation, develop
> in us to more precise observations and ideas and thereby bring to con-
> sciousness, in more stable observations and more general ideas, the defini-
> teness of emotional impressions. (vol. II, pp. 269–70)

Hegel, and later Gervinus, who, as mentioned above, despised and
disparaged program music (*Handel and Shakespeare*, p. 164),
intended that the argument should support a conviction of the su-
periority of vocal music. Brendel employed the same argument to
justify the symphonic poem, and his reinterpretation cannot be dismissed as a distortion. The same idea fits different interests, apolo-
getic or polemical. The adherents of program music in the
nineteenth century were enthusiasts of progress. They felt sure and
safe in their knowing that they had reckoned the intentions of the
world-spirit, and were in the process of fulfilling them. They
argued from the philosophy of history; their opponents argued
from psychology. Program music seemed to the progressives something historically 'necessary,' hence also possible; to their opponents it seemed empirically 'impossible,' hence superfluous or
injurious, an aberration of some high-falutin' esthetical speculation which was spilling over into composers' practice with dis-
astrous results. Effusions of philosophy of history confronted a
skepticism employing the technique of psychological unmasking.
The illusion that people on both sides spoke the same language,
that of esthetics, was deceptive. 'Esthetics,' the label for the controversy, was an empty word whose function consisted simply in
hiding the fact that people were talking at cross purposes in a dialogue gone askew.

The psychological argument, based on experimental evidence,
went off the track – to a point where no opponent the argument was
meant for could be found. Concerning the actual thing whose
esthetic right or wrong was at stake in the grounds of the quarrel,
nothing was so irrelevant as the attempt, repeated unceasingly and
always with negative results, to have listeners guess the program of

a work unknown to them. To begin with, an advocate of program music might have objected that the listeners' open minds were a handicap, though possibly an advantage to an experimental psychologist seeking natural laws of perception and association; for Liszt, one of the aims in view was to mediate between music and a traditional culture that was primarily literary and philosophical. An open mind – naive, unreflective listening – was just what ought to be extirpated from the musical public. Secondly, it is a crude misunderstanding to think that a program is the meaning of a symphonic poem, that the program could decode the music, as if it were a text in cipher.

In any attempt to sketch an esthetics adequate for program music, the ambiguity of the term 'content' gets in the way, yet there is no way around this category, however slippery it may be. In speaking about music the word 'content' designates sometimes a subject that exists outside music, at other times an ingredient of the musical work itself; only the second meaning is relevant for esthetics. To think that Liszt translated poems into music – that he tried to say in another language the same thing as the original text – is a mistake, but its absurdity never prevented its dissemination; even an esthetician as respectable as Gervinus succumbed to it. Of course Goethe's *Faust* is not the content of Liszt's 'Faust' Symphony but merely its subject. And a subject is no model to be imitated but rather a sort of material that the composer elaborates. A supply of tones and a subject, if we may simplify the point, constitute two kinds of material. Only from the interaction of subject and 'forms moved in sounding' does the musical content arise; a wish to narrate the content involves a misunderstanding about its mode of existence. If the subject specifies meanings for musical themes and motives, the opposite is equally valid: the broad significance and import of the subject is newly minted by the musical themes and motives. Program music rests on the interdependence of its components.

Despite such a defense of program music, the precarious esthetic situation of symphonic poems is not to be denied. But to emphasize this is uncalled for when the symphonic poem is a dead genre in any New Music worthy of the name, and when, above all, the symphonic poem faces our century's esthetic prejudices all lined up against it, if we disregard so-called 'socialist' esthetics. The position of symphonic poems in general musical consciousness may be characterized as an unhappy medium between no-longer and not-yet. Alienated from immediate understanding, they are not yet remote enough to be discovered and restored by historical understanding. The difference between absolute music and program music, as Walter Wiora (1963; see bibliography) has emphasized, is not exclusive opposition. There are countless transitional degrees between the extremes in musical reality. Merely because stark alternatives result from the simplification unavoidable in controversies, intermediate choices need not be forgotten. There is evidence that a program may be secret, either from esthetic conviction or to avoid criticism – good evidence in the cases of Haydn, Weber, Mahler, and even Bruckner. Indeed, even in Beethoven's symphonies and chamber music Arnold Schering sought esoteric programs, but if these existed they would still be irrelevant to esthetics: historical genesis of works is not the same as their esthetic value. Sometimes, not unlike the subjects in Liszt's symphonic poems, epigraphs appear for individual movements – another intermediate stage between absolute music and program music – to indicate particular aspects of the work's conception. But in other cases such epigraphs have been added later to prevent a listener's fantasy from straying in wrong directions. And, finally, a motto differs only slightly from designations of character, which often blur into prescriptions of tempo or articulation, without need for any sharp line of demarcation.

Program music, to oversimplify somewhat, is the music of an era when experience was shaped by reading and when literature on a subject was scarcely less important than the subject itself. And the zeal of nineteenth-century efforts to justify program music or even to declare it the goal of music history would be incomprehensible were it not for the interaction of esthetic and social motives. Liszt's theories can be deciphered as ideology, as justification, but of course the fact that an idea supports some particular interest does not prove that it is false.

The hopes placed in the symphonic poem betray insecurity with respect to the symphony. Although Beethoven's work was regarded with a reverence that gradually changed from bewildered awe to understanding, and although instrumental music had been praised as 'marvel of the art of tones' by the music enthusiasts among the Romantics – Wackenroder, Tieck, and E. T. A. Hoffmann – still as late as 1850 there was vitality in the idea, whose roots were centuries deep, that music was primarily vocal music. Whereas in the twentieth century the use of auxiliary texts or pictures to give music a meaning counts as a sign of dilettantism or even of musical stupidity (though the justice of this may be doubted), in the nineteenth century 'pure sounding,' as Hegel called it, was almost universally felt to be a difficult language – one sensed of course that it was eloquent but it kept eluding comprehension or any assurance about a content of the music. August Wilhelm Ambros (surely no dilettante) wrote in 1856: 'Of course everyone feels more or less, when faced with such works of tone' – he means Beethoven's symphonies – 'an awakening in himself of that "talent in sound-pictures" that Heine boasts of. This music, struggling with all its might, urges onward toward specific expressions; it is like an enchanted genie whose salvation depends on the uttering of some single word by the person it faces – the genie itself is not permitted to say the word and the person stands before it mute, puzzling, indeed searching with passionate eagerness for the right word' (*Die Grenzen der Musik*, p. 131).

Closely bound up with the esthetic motive urging onward toward program music, formulated so effectively by Ambros, was a social motive. Music, especially instrumental music, seemed, to the cultured individuals among the many who despised it, an art without tradition, an art of humble rank, which did not reach up to poetry. In the words of Hegel,

A composer, regarded momentarily from his own point of view, may of course endow his work with some specific meaning, some content of ideas and feelings and their complete articulate process; he may also, untroubled about such import, concern himself with the purely musical structure of his work and the intellectual wealth of such architectonics. But, from this latter point of view, his musical product can easily become something quite devoid of thought or feeling, which needs no awareness of culture or character, no matter how deep this consciousness may happen to have been otherwise. (*Aesthetics*, vol. II, p. 322)

Hegel's propositions, bespeaking barefaced contempt, were the expression of a common opinion felt as a challenge by Liszt, in whose esthetic theories more than a minor role is played by social motives. To the argument that music, incomplete in itself, had an inner tendency to turn into poetry or else serve as a foil for poetry, Liszt opposed his peremptory and provocative counterargument: 'Music in its masterpieces more and more incorporates the masterpieces of literature into itself' ('Berlioz and his Harold-Symphony,' *Gesammelte Schriften*, vol. IV, p. 58).

Liszt is like a usurper, grasping in the name of music what was poetry's property. His hybrid proclamation contradicts the spirit of the age, which was stamped by the predominance of literature. Yet by the same token, Liszt's statement, as a formula combining esthetics and philosophy of history, is imaginable in hardly any other time, for its hyperbolical tone is founded less on individual conceit than on the idiom of the decades of Hegel's greatest fame and immediate influence. Berlioz's program, which had been rejected by Schumann in his critique of the Fantastic Symphony as 'something undignified and quackish,' meant just the reverse for Liszt, Schumann's musical opposite: in Liszt's view the program was a means of establishing the dignity of instrumental music, its claim to be 'culture' and not merely 'enjoyment,' as Kant had scornfully maintained.

The bold pretension of the symphonic poem set it apart from older kinds of program music that had been content to be divertissements. At the same time, the pretension was prepared by the poeticizing criticism and hermeneutics of the early nineteenth century, whose influence on how music was listened to, and also on how composers practiced their craft, should not be underestimated. Consciousness of music is determined, to no small extent, by literature about music. Even people who scoff at it can hardly escape the effect of what is written. Musical experience almost always involves memory-traces from reading. And the meaning accumulated by music in its secondary, literary mode of existence does not leave untouched its primary mode, the realm of composition.

The idea that criticism was called upon to enter into the developmental process of art was part of the early Romantics' esthetic program. Moreover, criticism was to fulfill this mission not so much by judging the rank of works as by reflecting on their import. Novalis wrote: 'The business of an art critic is to find formulae for individual artists whereby they first become understood in any real sense. The critic's work prepares the history of art.' The idea of productive criticism, sharing in the definition of production itself, made its way into music literature a few decades later. It forms one of the central motives in Franz Brendel's defense of program music. Brendel, as mentioned above, saw in the 'unity of the poetic–musical,' as this unity was realized for him in Liszt's symphonic poems, the conscious final outcome of a tendency that had determined unconsciously and in rudimentary forms of expression the entire history of instrumental music. But the transition from latent to manifest, from the cunning of reason to the prominence of reason in the self-awareness of composers, was mediated by criticism, according to Brendel, who estimated his own place in history as no footnote. 'The essence of today's art consists above all in its no longer building further and further on given foundations in the old naturalistic way' – by which he means instinctive way – 'but on the contrary, in the intervention of theory and criticism between yesterday's and today's art, and in our art's presupposing theory and criticism within itself' (p. 624).

No matter how skeptical we may be of Brendel's synthetic history – his idea of a development from 'naturalism' to self-consciousness – still there is no denying the argument that one of the presuppositions of the symphonic poem was the poeticizing criticism whose paradigms had been supplied by E. T. A. Hoffmann and Schumann. It is hardly exaggerating to regard the symphonic poem as a musical realizing, by composers, of a literary principle that had determined descriptions and expositions of music ever since the beginning of the century. Liszt was not wrong to explain the conception of the symphonic poem as a consequence of the reception of Beethoven's music:

The attempts, becoming more and more frequent during the past fifteen years or so, to comment on Beethoven's symphonies, quartets, and sonatas, and to explain and fix in poetic and philosophical treatments the impressions they give us, the pictures they awaken in us – these attempts show how great is the need to see the guiding ideas of great instrumental works precisely designated. (*Gesammelte Schriften.*, vol. IV, pp. 24–5)

Viewing the history of the symphony as a prehistory of the symphonic poem (or of the music-drama, according to Wagner's theory) came to be a slogan for the Young Germans who issued their own manifesto as the party of progress. But the modernity represented by Berlioz and Liszt slowed, more than it fulfilled, the whole historical course of the previous century and a half, not with respect to techniques of composition, to be sure, but with respect to esthetics. In the development of listening to music, it is hardly possible to deny that a tendency has gradually prevailed to conceive vocal music in instrumental terms, as Schoenberg testified about himself, instead of searching in instrumental works for programs, whether explicit or secret. The role of the symphonic poem in the history of the emancipation of instrumental music is equivocal: progressive and regressive at once. The claim to rank as art in an emphatic sense, which Liszt put forward for Beethoven's instrumental works and for his own, was progressive. The methods whereby he tried to establish his claim were regressive: grasping for 'masterpieces of literature,' whose transfiguration into tones he thought would prove that music was an art not to be despised.

11

Tradition and reform
in opera

At the moment I decided to write an opera, I desired of course to make good music, to give musical fulfillment to the intellectual and spiritual content of Büchner's immortal drama [*Wozzeck*], to transpose his poetic language into a musical language; and apart from these wishes what haunted me was nothing, even in terms of the technique of composition, but the wish to give the theater what belongs to the theater. In other words, I intended to form music aware of its responsibility, at every moment, of serving the drama. Still more, to form music that produces everything this drama needs for transposing it to the reality of the stage – music that produces all this out of its own resources alone. Thereby my intention called on me, the composer, for all the essential tasks of an ideal *régisseur*. And all this without detriment to the otherwise absolute right to existence (purely musical right) of such a music; without detriment to its own life, which nothing extramusical should encumber.

Alban Berg in the title of his article 'The "problem of opera"' (1928) uses quotation marks to maintain his distance from the 'problem.' His article formulates the principles of music-drama, without the use of Wagner's vocabulary, although even Berg's *Wozzeck*, undeniably modern as it is in some respects, must be understood in relation to the tradition of Wagner's music-drama. The argument that in opera the music is obliged to 'serve the drama' – the argument of Wagner, or of Gluck – is taken for granted as if there were no more need to quarrel about it, as if one could not safely predict that a controversy centuries old would reach a conclusion only along with the controversy's object. Berg speaks also, with no embarrassment, of the theatrical function of musical 'ambience,' of the *mise en scène* through music, an aspect that Nietzsche* emphasized in order to denigrate it and turn it against Wagner. 'You see, I am essentially an anti-theatrical type; from the

---

* Friedrich Nietzsche (1844–1900) is as familiar to some readers as Dahlhaus counts on all German readers to be, but others may need reminders of his first book, *The birth of tragedy* (1872), dedicated to Wagner, of his disillusionment with Wagner, growing from 1876, when he read the libretto of *Parsifal*, and his *Thus spake Zarathustra* (1885).

bottom of my soul I feel a deep contempt for the theater, this mass-art *par excellence*; every artist today feels the same contempt' ('Nietzsche contra Wagner,' 1888, *Werke*, 1967, vol. II, p. 1041). Opera is a composite work, but not yet on that account a synthesis of all the arts (*Gesamtkunstwerk*). The inner 'synchronization of the arts,' proposed for them by philosophy of history, that is, that all arts together represent the same phase of development, has seldom or never been realized in opera. Even allowing a possibility that the spirit of the times, so far as such a thing exists, permeates all arts – and this possibility has been contested as often as maintained – still hardly anyone would deny that in opera the components or features have almost always been 'out of phase.' Even for an orthodox Wagnerian it must be hard to blink the fact that Wagner's imagination with respect to stage design lagged behind his musical imagination.

But what was unattainable – or seemed unattainable – meant a challenge, by which the history of opera was driven onward. Attempts were made again and again to convert the composite work of art into a synthesis. Moreover, of course, the supposition that it must be possible to forge together heterogeneous aspects into a homogeneous form drew nourishment from an idea that is something like an obsession – an *idée fixe* – in the history of opera: the dream of a revival or rebirth of ancient tragedy. Revolutions in opera were intended as restorations, as recovering of an 'age-old truth.' Wagner called this truth 'music-drama' in opposition to opera's lapsing into an incoherent agglomeration of stage spectacle and concert.

The history of opera, that 'impossible work of art' (Oscar Bie), seems to be a rare case of a development that can fit one of the oldest historiographical schemes, that of the origin, decline, and restoration of an idea. But what sort of notion of tragedy was it that provided the soil in which opera was rooted, then was left behind and sacrificed to the domination of sensuous singing and stage machinery, in order to be restored in the eighteenth century by Gluck, and again, after a second decay, restored in the nineteenth by Wagner? This notion of tragedy was a fiction: a typical case of fruitful misunderstanding. In the Camerata at Florence where toward 1600 attempts to reconstruct ancient drama intensified, historical information was simply insufficient, although these attempts were supported by a philologist as eminent as Girolamo Mei. And since little was known that was useful in practice, all the archeological reconstruction, taken so seriously, turned into its opposite: a modern genre of art with its own law of form, which law, against all attempts to conceive opera as drama, kept enforcing itself with quiet and unobtrusive power. This power may be either accepted as lying in the nature of the thing, or dismissed as mere momentum of convention. Perhaps all exertions which invoke 'true drama' in order to relegate music to a secondary role in opera are the ideological tradition of the genre, while the actual, more effective tradition is that of a theater 'born of the spirit of music,' a theater that need not be motivated dramatically through any dialectic of tragedy or comedy in order to win legitimacy. The thought of reestablishing the form of ancient tragedy was a chimera, and recognized as such in the nineteenth century, if not in the seventeenth and eighteenth. Yet Wagner never got free from the idea of tragedy. In his *Ring of the Nibelung* the Nordic mythology is crossed and recrossed with ancient motives, especially from Aeschylus. While this in itself is only an external indication, what is decisive is Wagner's conviction that it had to be possible to restore, if not the form, then still the effect of Greek tragedy. In Wagner's dream of Bayreuth, a dream whose realization appalled Nietzsche, the modern public transformed itself into a religious congregation. And the telling sign that distinguishes an orthodox Wagnerian from a heretical one is not so much his opinion about music as his belief in the religious character of a performance of *Parsifal* or even the *Ring*.

The thought that renewing ancient drama was the basic idea of opera, the origin and aim of its history, has a more pallid variant: the thesis that the various attempts to establish precedence for text over music are the progressive features of opera history. The reforming programs of the eighteenth and nineteenth centuries – Gluck's and Wagner's polemics against a tradition charged with having become sloppy – rested on the conviction that operatic singing was a kind of elevated declamation, in a way of speaking or chanting that went back to the 'original language of mankind,' and that music ought to be related intelligibly to the text at every moment, in order to fulfill the demands of musical drama. It is a fact, however, that musical language has been enriched and further differentiated by the pressure imposed on it to follow a text to the last detail, and this fact need not be set aside in order permissibly to maintain that nothing has worked more confusingly in opera esthetics than the habit of regarding drama and text as the same thing. The formula 'word and tone,' though Wagner's authority stands behind it, is the ruin of opera interpretation, to put it in broad terms. Nothing is more mistaken than to assume that the text represents the dramatic aspect of an opera, so that an opera will be more dramatic the greater the privileges it hands over to the text. For what can be called in opera its dramatic or theatrical meaning is not to be read off from a mere text, but rather takes definition only from the juncture of music, language, scenery, and stage movement and gesture. This juncture may become a dialectic or even a counterpoint, in which the text often plays only a slight role. To confuse theater with declamation is the elementary fallacy of dramaturgy. More decisive than words, in opera, is the visible and palpable situation from which the words grow.

It seems as if only one trait is ascribed to drama by all estheticians, even if they quite thoroughly contradict each other: this trait is drama's antithetical character. But antithesis is a concept comprehending an unsurveyable multiplicity of possibilities, from bald, blatant contrast to complex dialectics. It hardly needs saying that simple obvious contrast is one of the leading categories of opera. It may be more noteworthy that contrasts that shirk the category of dramatic-theatrical form run the risk of serving as a mere directorial device to gratify musical consumers with the charm of variety. It would probably not be unrewarding to analyze Meyerbeer's operas from points of view that have intruded on us from the modern entertainment industry, whose prehistory extends back into the nineteenth century.

Nietzsche turned away from opera, the sensational theater, as 'mass-art *par excellence*,' and indeed all attempts to ennoble opera by some intricate dialectics are thwarted by its ineradicable tendency toward exaggeration. The expression 'dialectics' means, if understood in Hegel's sense, that something must be analyzed into opposing phases in order to arrive at the thing itself or to win recognition as what it is. In its first, immediate form, its essence is still hidden. Only a development – an unrolling process – by way of antithesis allows the essence to come to the fore. Dialectics conceived in this way is unmistakably analogous to the structure of a sonata movement, whose themes are taken apart in the development section, in order to reappear in the recapitulation richer by distinguishable motives and inner relationships than the same themes were in the exposition. But in opera or music-drama narrow limits are set to the musical development of thoughts, despite Wagner's claim that the symphony was 'transcended' in the music-drama. A motive or theme in an opera must not be referred to a development whereby its import becomes intelligible, but rather must show at once in its exposition what it is all about. Only the present counts; this is one of the laws of operatic music. The excess of meaning accumulated by Wagner's 'guiding motives' in the course of the works is due less to musical development than to dramatic development. The limitation of musical dialectics in opera is balanced by possibilities which are implied by the collaboration and conflict of heterogeneous components. Since opera is a composite form of art, novelty – the driving force of historical development – may be founded on the music as well as on the text, the scenery, or the relations among the various components. It would be wrong to expect that a new direction in opera, to be revolutionary, always had to rest on some profound change of musical language, or even had just to coincide with such a change. The kind of opera made by Bertolt Brecht and Kurt Weill was undeniably progressive around 1930. The accident that external intervention cut short any unfolding of this operatic type after a few years does not invalidate its claim to have been revolutionary. But to draw the consequence that the music of *Mahagonny* or the *Threepenny Opera* must count as progressive on its own would be mistaken. Brecht did indeed change the relations between text and music. But he left intact the public's habit of feeling more conventional musical responses in opera than at a concert; he even exploited this habit. Against the conception of a synthesis of the arts, in which Wagner hoped the single arts would fit together without contradiction and work together for the same purpose, Brecht posed the idea of a musical theater in which text, music, 'gestics,' and scenery mutually intercut and 'alienate' each other. Alienation is supposed to make striking what is ordinary; our everyday behavior, which seems to us universally human and hence natural, as if there were no other way to behave, is to be shown as strange, surprising, and modifiable. The universally human, according to Brecht, is nothing other than the mask of a historical situation wretched enough to justify the resolve to change it.

The slogan of popular esthetics, that music is a universal language, suggests that any situation grasped in tones becomes available for feeling as a universally human situation. Brecht takes the slogan literally, but he employs it with a critical intention. When he alienates a tune attesting fine emotions by joining it with a text betraying mean thoughts, Brecht seeks to demonstrate that the emotions, the universally human, are mere masks for selfish interest. But, to be useful for alienation by a text, the music must work just as conventionally as the emotions that it represents. In other words, the music in itself, to be able to play its role in a progressive work of art, must be precisely regressive – every bit as sentimental as popular esthetics claims it is. Nature and function split apart.

Reversing the relationships between text and music in Brecht, it is also possible for a new musical language to combine with an older form of opera. Schoenberg's music in *Moses and Aaron* is separated from Wagner by a historical rupture so profound that one more profound can hardly be imagined; though the beginnings of Schoenberg's music reach back into Wagnerian tradition, the later separation could not be missed by any listener. At the same time, Schoenberg, just like Berg, undeniably took over almost unchanged the idea of music-drama, the principle that music is a means serving the purpose of drama. Although Schoenberg's ideas about the connection between text and music were thus enmeshed in traditional ideas, his musical language goes far beyond what might be expected according to the literal dictates of his own opera esthetics. It is a mistake to think that Schoenberg's music can be disposed of as fag-end Romanticism; presumably this mistake, insofar as it is not mere neo-classicist ideology, motivated by wishing to clear a way for some new would-be classic, is based to a considerable extent on taking Schoenberg's esthetics too literally and understanding his music too inexactly. Just as in Brecht's conception of opera, even though with reversed positions, something progressive and something traditional are interlocked. And the contradiction is no inert one; rather it is productive.

12

Esthetics and history

To regard works of art as primary documents and to wish to exert every means for the purpose of reading and interpreting them correctly, above all, without regard to esthetic enjoyment, this I see as one of the most important steps forward in recent times.

This programmatic statement by Philipp Spitta was written in 1893, a year before his death, in *Die Grenzboten* (*News from the frontier*), justifying the publication of the multi-volumed *Denkmäler deutscher Tonkunst* (*Monuments of the German art of tones*).

Spitta, next to August Wilhelm Ambros, was the most significant music historian of the nineteenth century. His statement separates history and esthetics with an abruptness that might be understood as fending off an onerous difficulty. Spitta postulates precise and unalterable distinctions between esthetics and history, which are meant to guard judgments in each field from adulteration. As an object of esthetic enjoyment, as Spitta calls it, a musical work is not a primary document concerning the state of fugal technique in the early eighteenth century, or the spirit of pietism in music, but rather nothing but itself, transcending time, and cut away from the accidental conditions out of which it arose. Vice versa, as soon as it is analyzed as a historical document, as evidence concerning states of affairs outside itself, it is extinguished as a work of art. Thus, if the argument is carried to an extreme, there emerges the possibility of an 'art history without art.' For Spitta, writing history is dominated by the idea of development, while the supreme category of esthetics is contemplation, in which a beholder or listener forgets himself and all the world. For Spitta, an attempt to unite the *disjecta membra* of historical investigation on the one hand and of esthetic enjoyment on the other would be suspect; such an attempt might be an arbitrary or confused mixing of irreconcilable things. Moreover, the late nineteenth century emphasized the division and difference between disciplines especially as part of its effort to detach itself from the epoch of 'art religion,' the age of Goethe and Hegel, when connections among disciplines had seemed promising; the new Positivist age insisted on infallible scientific rigor. For Winckelmann and Herder, esthetics and history intermingled. In the decades around 1800, these two disciplines, concerning themselves with particular individual things, were set apart from a rationalistic dogmatism that measured both past and present by invariable norms of nature and reason. Esthetics and history focussed on what was unrepeatable; they upheld the right of exceptions to the rule or of departure from what was general and recurrent. The distinctions of method, which Spitta later exaggerated, hardly occurred to people in the first enthusiasm of discovering the individual.

Bringing these distinctions into the open was doubtless, as Spitta expressed it, 'one of the most important steps forward in recent times.' To be sure, historical judgments about music deal with the same objects as esthetic judgments, but they grasp the objects in a different way, as if from the reverse side. Anyone who feels the subject of a Bach fugue as beautiful or sublime makes a legitimate esthetic judgment even if he does not know who originated the melody, nor know the fact that this melody is a variant of a type whose prehistory stretches back into the early seventeenth century. Esthetic experience is apparently independent of historical knowledge, or at least may be so.

Yet the two sides, which Spitta sharply separated from each other on principle, zealous as he was for scientific rigor and suspicious of dialectics, are in fact closely connected with each other. More exact analysis shows that historical knowledge is quite often founded on esthetic judgment, as well as vice versa. Art history must be reckoned among the historical disciplines; it takes its bearings from their methods; but this fact does not exclude another: that art history is forced to accept from esthetics its object of study. An esthetic judgment, whether explicit or not, is inherent in the decision as to whether a piece of music is to be accepted as art or may be left out of account, as not art. The canon of classics, and of old masters, is more a presupposition of art history than a resultant.

Conversely, many esthetic judgments are established by way of historical judgments. No one denies that the significance of a musical work of the nineteenth or twentieth century – its 'substantial import,' as Hegel would say – diminishes or even disappears if the work is seen through as derivative, for an esthetic sense of tact bristles at a composer's stealing another's language, as it were. But to admit that originality or its absence is an esthetic criterion implies that there are esthetic experiences that include historical knowledge and would be impossible without it, no matter how slight or subordinate its role.

The esthetic or partly esthetic character of a judgment that some work is derivative cannot be doubted: this judgment cannot be conceived as either merely historical or as exclusively a matter of techniques of composition. Anyone who confined himself strictly within a historian's limits might of course establish that a piece of music repeated something said earlier, but such a historian could not speak about derivativeness as a shortcoming. Yet the judgment that a work lacks originality cannot be securely founded purely on considerations of technique without regard for the time of composition, which is a historical factor. Again, an immaculate copy of style is imaginable, no matter that it may rarely or never occur; and however perfect it might be, just so unavoidably would it fall under the verdict of being derivative and therefore esthetically worthless. In the accusation of derivativeness, historical and esthetic aspects are inseparably interlocked.

The criterion of originality, however, on which this accusation is based, is itself historically limited. Its validity does not extend back before the eighteenth century. To say that a sixteenth-century motet was derivative would be beside the point, since in that century imitating model composers was viewed as a legitimate procedure. Moreover it is not out of the question, though it seems improbable, that imitation, suspect up to now, will be rehabilitated sooner or later. For the esthetics to which the criterion of originality belongs is a historical phenomenon itself; it arose in the eighteenth century and its duration cannot be predicted.

Kant speaks in the *Critique of judgment* about the 'teleological' judgment concerning the function of a structure. What he says about it – that it serves 'as foundation and condition' for esthetic judgment if the object judged is a work of art – may be maintained for historical judgment too, by analogy, and with equal justice. If some listener is unable to date a melody of arpeggiated triads as early classical period and therefore dismisses it as jejune, this listener is just as mistaken as another listener who complains of the lack of melodiousness in a fugue subject, instead of recognizing it as a fugue subject and judging, accordingly, as to whether it fulfills its function or not. Of course an esthetic judgment, simply hailing some object as beautiful, represents very little judgment based on knowledge; but this is no more self-limiting than the opinion, which comes from misunderstanding the *Critique of judgment*, that intellectual aspects, either teleological or historical, disturb and confuse esthetic judgment. Intellectual aspects, to be sure, are merely 'foundation and condition,' not goal and result of esthetic contemplation; but they are scarcely dispensable as presuppositions, if esthetic experience is not to remain impoverished and insubstantial. 'Immediacy' may be an attribute of esthetic intuition, but it is not so devoid of presuppositions as is wished by the apologists for the kind of naiveté that transcends itself by proclaiming itself naive, reflecting on itself, and bristling at intellectual sneers. It is not so much a starting-point as a point of arrival: 'mediated immediacy,' to speak in the idiom of Hegel. One of the mediating components, moreover, is historical knowledge. A 'purely' esthetic experience, appreciating in some object nothing but its beauty, is a thin abstraction. Kant's emphasis is a matter of method and logic, not founded in the nature of experience. What for him is the decisive aspect, 'culture,' he attributes more readily to 'accessory' beauty than to 'free' beauty.

Unabridged esthetic experience implies something historical. This is shown negatively in the incomprehension or misunderstanding encountered by music from a remote period, such as the fourteenth century. Esthetic contemplation is not entirely independent of this remoteness: it can be influenced by it or even prevented by it. (It may not be unheard of that a listener enjoys something he does not comprehend precisely because it remains uncomprehended, but this may be considered a peripheral phenomenon, if not to say quite irrelevant.) What is obvious with things remote in time or space, however, is equally true, though less strikingly so, even with works closer to us, which require for understanding no perceptible exertion. A commentary – going to the trouble of historical reflection – is superfluous only because we take for granted the intellectual and historical features of the work. And our taking them for granted is what misleads us into overlooking them, to succumbing to an illusion that esthetic appreciation is 'immediate and without presuppositions.' Those historical mediations that serve as 'foundation and condition' for a symphony of Brahms or a music-drama of Wagner remain hidden, because they have been worn down to traditions that we do not reflect on. But in fact they do still exert an effect, and our esthetic experience would be enriched if we were aware of them. That the 'second immediacy' represents the goal of esthetic conduct should not be abused as an argument to justify the 'first immediacy.' For people who claim the first, it is generally nothing but an alibi for obtuseness. Absorption in a work of art, no matter how self-forgetful, is seldom a mystical state in a literal sense, seldom a motionless and hallucinatory fixation. More likely it is a to-and-fro between contemplating and reflecting, and, if so, then the level it reaches depends on the esthetic and intellectual experiences contributed by the listener, experiences into whose context he can fit the work that he is now appreciating. Intellectual features are no superfluous addenda; rather they are always an intrinsic part of esthetic perception. They may of course take forms either rudimentary or highly developed, and there is no reason to suppose that any esthetic advantage is gained from keeping these features in a primitive condition. Shying away from concepts is hardly a warrant for or a badge of esthetic sensitivity.

13

Toward the
phenomenology of music

1.

So what is time? If no one asks me, I know; if I am to explain it to someone asking, then I do not know. (Quid est ergo tempus? Si nemo ex me quaerat, scio, si quaerenti explicare velim, nescio.)

Internal contradictions in the concept of time made Augustine philosophically ill-at-ease (*Confessions*, Bk XI, chap. 17). These contradictions do not leave music untouched – music being the 'art of time *par excellence*' (Gisèle Brelet). Is the present – now – the only reality of time, between what is no longer and what is not yet? Or is the present just the opposite, a mere boundary line between past and future, nothing in itself, an aspect that passes as it arrives? For Augustine, a tone or a syllable can pose the puzzle; is it irresolvable? Edmund Husserl avoids it by understanding the 'present' as no fleeting punctual now, but rather as a stretch of time whose extent depends on the duration of a process that fills it up, a process felt as cohering without a break.

A whole melody seems present as long as it is still sounding, as long as tones are sounding that belong to the melody, intended in a single perceptive context. (*The phenomenology of internal time-consciousness*, 'Vorlesungen zur Phänomenologie des inneren Zeitbewusstseins,' in *Jahrbücher zur Philosophie und phänomenologische Forschung*, vol. IX, 1928, p. 398)

In the concept or intuition of *temps durée*, 'experienced' time, passing not in an even flow but alternately fast and hesitating, Henri Bergson sought to reconstruct the original experience of time, which precedes *temps espace*, time spatially represented. Since Bergson, the claim is made fairly often that music is a form of appearance of *temps durée*, a sounding Gestalt of *temps durée*. But the features that Bergson rigidly separated arise in experience not isolated from each other, but rather bound together by their interaction. If *temps espace*, empty before and after, is abstracted from *temps durée*, it is no less the case that the stretchings and

74

shortenings of experienced time can be felt only against a background of spatial time. And both aspects, *temps espace* and *temps durée*, are at work in music, as temporal framework and movement.

Going beyond Bergson, we might ask: is time a mere medium of processes in it? or is time itself an occurrence, which advances from the past into the present or approaches the present from the future? And does music situate itself 'in time' or does music rather have 'time in itself'? This question has been answered variously in the literature about musical time, a literature in which surplus rather than shortage prevails; in their various answers, disputants are insufficiently aware that they use the word 'music' in various meanings. At all events, the contradiction between arguments may be resolved by assuming that some writers mean a repeatable musical work, while others mean a work's unrepeatable individual performances. According to Roman Ingarden, sounding music is a 'real' object, notated music a 'purely intentional' object (*Untersuchungen zur Ontologie der Kunst, Investigations of the ontology of art*, 1962, p. 101). And the characteristics of the temporal structure correspond to the characteristics of the object. The duration of a single performance is a bit of real, unrepeatable time. By contrast, a duration is immanent in a notated work, a duration specified by the extension and succession of parts. This latter duration, just like the 'purely intentional object' to which it belongs as one aspect, has no place in real, unrepeatable time. The notated work is not tied to any here and now, but rather can be repeated. Hence the single performances, 'realizations' of a work, may be 'contained in time,' while the notated work may be described, precisely in reverse, as 'containing time,' and the work intended by notation is the 'work itself,' recurring as identical in all its performances, no matter how different they are as acoustical 'realizations.' The fact, moreover, of a one-way passage from immanent duration toward real duration makes no change in the difference between the forms of time.

The commonplace statement that music is a 'shaping of time' (*Zeitgestalt*) or 'shaped time' (*gestaltete Zeit*) leaves open a question about the inner unity of a structure of tones. (And sometimes this unity seems to be subjected, by the constant use of the word 'Gestalt,' to the exclusive expertise of the school of psychology for which this term is a label.) The question is to what degree the inner unity is grasped and constituted passively and receptively on the one hand, and on the other to what extent it is grasped by a conscious, spontaneous activity of assembling, comparing, and relating. No firm agreement exists as to whether Gestalt psychology, whose experimentally based insights belong to the realm of psychology of perception, must be entrusted with determining what a *Zeitgestalt* is and is not. It seems as though the criteria of psychology of perception may indeed suffice for describing impressions of tonal structures with brief extent, but not for explaining musical coherences extending over a longer time. The term 'Gestalt,' transferred to a whole sonata movement, is an empty word or else an expression of resentment toward analysis; some devotees of the 'Gestalt' would forbid musical analysis as an overreaching of reason into supposedly irrational things.

Musical perception that reaches beyond the grasp of isolated acoustical data would be unthinkable if data immediately past were not preserved. This preservation Husserl designated as 'retention'; its complementary opposite he called 'protention,' the expectation and anticipation of something future. Although at the end of a melodic period its beginning is no longer available for inspection, still we are sufficiently aware of the beginning for the melody to appear as a unit, a closed course of events: in musical ideas the present conclusion and the past beginning seem to stand beside each other more nearly than they contrast with each other in the way a looming figure contrasts against a faded ground. By means of 'retention' there arises something like an extended present. The point in time – now – stretches out to a line. Again, something immediately perceived often reminds us of something earlier, similar or the same, separated from the present by a shadowy span of time now sunk in oblivion. Continuity and discontinuity of musical hearing interpenetrate. While parts that in the course of a work have protruded as present and then been preserved by retention may coalesce in a continuum, the memory that relates a motive now present to a motive rather far in the past, as its return or variant, works sporadically and discontinuously. But both components mingle – the uninterrupted momentum that musically represents the flowing of time and the connection of what is remote. These components do not become confused but rather mutually condition and support each other. The bold leaps of memory, which Wagner counts on in his technique of guiding motives, not only break through the continuum but at the same time presuppose it as their supporting ground. And correspondingly something past, withdrawn from immediate retention, is preserved from being totally forgotten by recurrences of single motives, which evoke their musical surroundings into recollection at each recurrence.

The connection, however, between a motivic variant, occupying the present, and the model it recalls is not 'open to inspection.' The two motives are not 'side by side' in the same sense as two phrases may be called 'adjacent,' when the first half of a period, held firm by retention, is imagined as lying in a *temps espace* resulting from its original *temps durée* 'next to' the second half, now present. Rather, the model motive is grasped by way of the variant. The model remains 'abstract,' since it would be absurd to think of the motives as if acoustically 'superimposed,' as in a photographic double exposure. The model is paler than an image retained in memory. Moreover the relation as such is clearer for consciousness than the image to which the relation connects; the fact of similarity between model and variant is clearer than the motive announced to begin with, from which the motive heard now is derived. The general existence of some connection is more striking than what specifically is being connected with what. What is recalled, now evoked and made conscious again, is localized in the present, but at the same time it carries the tint of the past from which it comes. The times are locked together.

2.

Music is objective and yet it isn't. A musical work differs from primitive, aimless singing. This sort of singing ends but does not conclude; no one can foresee when it will break off. But a musical work presents a completed structure; even a listener unacquainted with it knows, *a priori*, that it is intended and ought to be grasped as a whole, with firm boundaries and definite articulations. Moreover, the expectation of unity in variety belongs to the thing itself, no matter how vague may be this expectation. It belongs to the intentional object, to speak the language of phenomenology. To be sure, the fact that the single perceptions, as they overlap, remain connected, instead of merely supplanting one another, results on the one hand from a comprehension that is partly receptive, partly spontaneous: the tones fit together in motives, the motives in periods, the periods in forms of movements. Yet, on the other hand, any listener accustomed to artificial music always presupposes the wholeness of a work, even a work quite unknown; and such a listener grasps details as parts of an expected coherence that includes the details and still proceeds from them.

A musical work is not altogether different from a visible object: the supposed whole of a musical work, anticipated in empty or weakly determinate expectation, resembles a visible whole, first presented in a vague over-all impression, then gradually defined more precisely by way of the individual features discerned one after another by the beholder. Although it would be perverse to blur or evade the difference between an acoustical process, extending in time, and spatially presented things – the category of 'object' has been abstracted from things (ob-jecta) tossed in the way of a subject (the German *Gegenstand* means a thing that stands opposite, or in the way of, a subject) – still it is undeniable that musical listening proceeds from the idea of a closed shape to which details are related as if they were features defining what underlies them. The anticipated whole is analogous to the visibly presented whole, and the anticipation may be more nearly defined by a title, announcing the whole, as representative of a type – sonata-form or rondo – so that a system of relations is specified in advance, and the listener's expectation can fasten on to it.

Insofar as musical works of art are grasped as such – not merely drifted through as if they were potpourris – each detail, just perceived, exists not for its own sake but rather as a component of some whole that listeners consciously anticipate. While a listener is discerning individual parts, his esthetic interest – elaborating and realizing itself through the experience of the details – always aims partially or even primarily at the comprehensive form. Details must be grasped as functions of the whole form, in order to attain unimpaired musical reality.

3.

No one seems to doubt the received opinion that music is sounding motion. The experience that music is motion forms the point of departure for several twentieth-century music estheticians, who are called 'energeticists' by Rudolf Schäfke, in his *Geschichte der Musikästhetik in Umrissen* (*History of music esthetics in outline*, 1934, p. 394), since these estheticians, borrowing partly from phenomenology and partly from metaphysics, trace back to a hypothetical energy the impression of motion produced by successions of tones. This energy, called 'will' by August Halm and 'power' by Ernst Kurth, is said to be effective in music as an agent and to constitute its hidden essence. The idea of a motion does indeed arise in listening to music, but however unavoidable this idea may be, it is nonetheless difficult to describe and analyze without falling into the confusing, stupefying language of Ernst Kurth, a language in which psychological and music-theoretical insights are mixed with metaphors drawn partly from physics and partly from vitalistic philosophy.

The phenomenon of motion is closely connected with that of tonal space: an unreal space, which must be distinguished from two other spaces, according to Albert Wellek, in his *Musikpsychologie und Musikästhetik*, 1963, Appendix. There is the real physical space in which music as sound can be located, on the one hand, and, on the other, there are ideas of space such as are evoked by the content of many works of program music. The custom of speaking about tonal space is rooted in ordinary colloquial language, not only in professional jargon. But the dimensions that constitute tonal space, its determining aspects, apparently symbolized by the vertical and horizontal dimensions of notation, are not unequivocal, either in their essence or in their relations to each other. Are the differences between tones 'distances,' spatially imaginable? Does it make sense to characterize as two 'dimensions' the pitch-interval and the duration of tones and to put these 'dimensions' into perpendicular relation with each other? This is not so obvious as some naive listener may suppose, for whom the terminology and notation of European music have come to be second nature in his way of perceiving tones.

To be sure, tones are felt to be high and low, as unprejudiced observation shows, but they are felt also as bright and dark. Moreover, in antiquity, both Greeks and Romans designated tones as sharp and heavy. (The question may be left unsettled whether those feelings are a matter of associations or of characteristics belonging to the thing itself.) Thus, while it would be erroneous to dismiss the idea of a vertical in tonal space as mere fiction, suggested by notation, still it should be undeniable that this idea combines conventional aspects with natural data. To perceive tones primarily as high and low, not bright and dark, is a result of emphasizing one of the possibilities of perception included in the phenomenon.

Hardly less problematical is the habit of referring to time as a second dimension of tonal space – and the time itself, indeed, is spatially imagined, *temps espace*. For time and all musical processes occurring in time are irreversible, but reversibility of directions belongs among the characteristics of a dimension in the strict sense of the word.

Again, how easily can any motion be imagined without some

carrier of the motion? But musical motion seems to lack any moving agent or substance. For it would be a questionable hypothesis to claim that it was a tone that moved in tonal space. A higher tone following a lower one is 'another' tone rather than 'the same' tone in another place. The first tone, when the melody proceeds, does not change its position, but is replaced, displaced by a second tone. Yet Ernst Kurth's attempt to hypostasize the motive energy that 'streams through' music as a living being, and to demote tones to mere points of transition, is too arbitrary and also too deeply enmeshed in metaphysics to be a convincing last word on the matter.

Perhaps the difficulties hindering any attempt to describe and analyze tonal space and musical motion – difficulties that often appear labyrinthine – might be overcome only by proceeding from the hypothesis that in the complex of impressions of space and motion what counts as primary is rhythm, not melody, as Kurth assumed. Rhythmic motion, determined in common-practice meters (*Taktrhythmik*) by the duration, stress, and character of the beats in a measure, is independent of melody, or at least may be independent, but melodic motion is not separable from rhythmic motion. One can think a rhythm without any succession of tones, but not a succession of tones without some rhythm. This indicates that rhythm forms the basic component of the impression of musical motion. Time – *temps durée* made into a firm *temps espace* – is the primary dimension of tonal space; verticality is secondary.

Assuming that precedence is given to rhythm, we may begin to understand a phenomenon that is hard to explain as long as independence from rhythm is claimed for a dimension of pitch, that is, for the impression that differences between tones are distances. It has often been observed that when tones sound together in chords the individual intervals' characteristic of distance or space is weakly manifest or even cancelled. This might be either because the characteristic is concealed and repressed by the tint of consonance or dissonance, or because it is only rudimentarily present in simultaneity, regardless of any such tint. One writer on the psychology of tones, Géza Révész, even denies that the characteristic of distance exists with simultaneous intervals. Only in succession is there a clear impression of a distance between tones – of some vertical aspect as a dimension of tonal space. But the fact, formulated cautiously, that with chords the manifestation of any characteristic of distance or space is less than with successions of tones – this fact might be most simply explained by the hypothesis that the idea of tonal space represents an abstraction from the phenomenon of musical motion, and that the basic aspect of this motion, from which others are dependent, is the rhythmic aspect. The vertical aspect – the impression that differences among tones are spatially representable distances – emerges only together with the horizontal. And since, in the case of a simultaneous interval, motion and rhythm drop out, the impression of distance or space is reduced as well, or even, if Révész wins assent, extinguished.

4.

Concerning music's phenomenological structure, Roman Ingarden developed a thesis in his polemic against Nicolai Hartmann, stating that music is 'one-levelled' while literature is 'multi-levelled' (*The literary work of art, Das literarische Kunstwerk*, 2nd edn, 1960, p. 35). This distinction, however, is brittle. To speak of levels of a work, according to Ingarden, makes sense only if the elements constituting a level satisfy three conditions: first, they are constitutive for all works of the art that is to be characterized; second, they form for themselves a coherence persisting through the whole work; and third, they are clearly distinguishable from elements of other levels. Ingarden accuses Hartmann of confusing the situation with his divergent terminology. Ingarden's three criteria may be designated more simply, without his own nomenclature, as those of (1) universality, (2) continuity of a level in itself, and (3) heterogeneity with respect to other levels. In literary works, with which Ingarden first and most significantly elaborated his theory and terminology, three levels are text (*Wortlaut*, which must be distinguished from the phonetic material that realizes the text in speaking), meaning, and represented object.

Ingarden, rightly no doubt, distinguishes between performances of a musical work, individual and always differing, and the work itself that remains 'the same' in all the modifications to which it submits. The identity intended and guaranteed by the name *Eroica* or Third Symphony is not cancelled by the diversity of interpretations in which the one composition assumes real sounding form. The work is a 'purely intentional' object, withdrawn from time, while a single performance is real and tied to the here-and-now. Furthermore, according to Ingarden, the truth about traits depending on interpretation – details of articulation and agogics or gradations of *forte* and *piano* – is that such traits do not belong to the work itself; thus they form no level. (The principle is unaffected by the fact that boundaries between composition and interpretation are historically variable, that a modern score represents the latest phase of a development whose first phase was the notation of mere scaffoldings of tonal structures.) To characterize music as 'one-levelled' is not arbitrary. Yet it can be refuted, even without referring to Nicolai Hartmann's usage of terms and arguments, through an immanent critique that confines itself within the limits of Ingarden's assumptions. Differences exist in a musical work between composition or tonal structure (*Tonsatz*) and sonorous form (*Klangform*), between quantity and quality, structure and function, similar to the differences between levels of a literary text; the similarity, however, does not warrant applying the metaphorical term, the word 'level,' to musical reality.

The sonorous form of a musical work, its particular instrumentation, has been part of its composition since the seventeenth or eighteenth century – the historical development completed itself sooner in some genres, later in others – while in earlier epochs sonorous form was a matter of performance practice. As an aspect of the work itself, moreover, sonorous form is separable from individual, particular reproductions of the work. This distinction is hardly different from that between the text (written or memorized *Wortlaut*) that forms one of the levels of a literary work (*Text*) and the variable phonetic material in which it is realized. If, then, the instrumentation belongs to the musical text, it is still distinguished clearly enough from the tonal structure (*Tonsatz*) to make possible its consideration as a level on its own, analogous to the literary text (*Wortlaut*). A tonal structure can be conceived without reference to sonorous form, and the instrumentation can be changed without any need to tamper with the structure of such a work. Tonal structure and sonorous form, in this view, would be two levels of a musical work satisfying Ingarden's conditions of universality, continuity of a level in itself, and heterogeneity with respect to other levels.

The distinction between musical quality and quantity may be understood analogously. Qualities, either of harmony and melody or of rhythm, are founded on quantities, without being reducible to quantities. Gradations of consonance and dissonance would be mere abstractions except for the intervals in which they are displayed. But consonance and dissonance, on the other hand, differ from the intervals, their foundation. Interval as quantity and gradation of consonance or dissonance as quality are heterogeneous in a manner like that of text and meaning in language.

What is called musical rhythm is a complex of phenomena or component parts. In this complex, qualities and functions involve each other inseparably. Deciding whether a measure's center of gravity is a matter more of quality or of function would be difficult, if not quite arbitrary. But the difference between qualities or functions and the fundamental quantities, the measurable traits, is unmistakable. For the same quality or function – a measure's center of gravity – may be expressed by various quantities: by modification of duration or of intensity. Whereas in a march or dance it may be appropriate to mark the center of gravity with an accent of intensity, in an organ piece the center cannot be made recognizable otherwise than through a slight agogic lengthening, which is not to strike a listener as lengthening but rather is to be perceived qualitatively. The variability of representation, however, is the sign of a heterogeneity that may be conceived as a difference between 'levels.' Musical rhythm, contrary to Ingarden's argument, is 'many-levelled.'

Finally there is no mistaking the divergence between a chord as sounding structure and the function, in harmony and tonality, that it fulfills in the context of a musical work from the eighteenth or nineteenth century. Hugo Riemann, most rigorous theoretician of tonal harmony, ascribes the same meaning in the context of C major, that of subdominant, to two chords: f-a-c, and f-a flat-d flat, which are drastically different externally, in their array of tones. Structure and function split apart.

. The image of levels can represent the aspects that Ingarden discriminates from each other in literature – text, meaning, and objective reference. But subjecting musical differences to the same metaphorical scheme is unsatisfactory, although an attempt to refute in Ingarden's own terms his argument that music is 'one-levelled' has compelled us to treat the differences between tonal structure and sonorous form, quantity and quality, structure and function as musical analogues to the levels of a literary text. Within rhythm, the split can be described better by the concepts of quantity and quality; in harmony, however, by the categories of structure and function; yet there seems to be no intelligible possibility either of identifying quality with function or of putting them on 'levels' one above the other. But no matter how futile the wish to count the 'levels' of a musical work, it is no less certain that calling music 'one-levelled' is mistaken.

14

Standards of criticism

There are two kinds of esthetics, altogether different from each other, and they must not be so confused as to make one a reproach to the other. The first is sensuous judgment, a cultivated natural ability to see perfection and imperfection in things of beauty and to enjoy them sensuously, hence vitally, hence thoroughly, hence rapturously. While all this is true, still the first esthetics always remains sensuous enjoyment, confused feeling, and it ought to remain so. Such talented souls we call geniuses, refined intelligences, people of taste. According to the degree to which they possess it, their esthetics is nature, good evidence in affairs of beauty. But what about the other esthetics, the really scientific esthetics? This applies its keen attention to the antecedent feelings, tears one part from the rest, abstracts parts from the whole – no longer a beautiful whole; for the moment, it is a beauty torn to pieces and mutilated. Then this esthetics proceeds through the several parts, reflects, brings all of them together again, in order to restore the previous impression, and finally compares. The more exactly it reflects, the more keenly it compares, so much the more firmly will it grasp beauty. Thus an articulate concept of beauty is no longer a self-contradiction, but rather a completely, utterly different thing from the confused feeling of beauty.

Herder, attempting to justify psychological–esthetic analysis (*Sämtliche Werke*, vol. IV, p. 24), rests his attempt on the idea of subordinating esthetics to a principle of faculties of the mind (*Gewaltenteilung*). Immediate feeling and intuition, 'sensuous, hence vital, hence thorough, hence rapturous,' grasp a work as a whole, but they loiter on a stage of development designated as 'confused' by Herder, just as it is by Alexander Baumgarten. The term 'confused' (*verworren*) means, in eighteenth-century academic philosophical language, that an impression lacks concepts and reflection, but this does not exclude its being a fairly 'clear' (*klar*) impression. The opposite of 'confused' is another word for 'clear,' 'articulate,' 'distinct' (*deutlich*); articulate ideas are mediated only by analysis, using concepts; in analysis, the whole, which constituted the basic data for the recipient's feelings and intuition, must be dissected; analysis 'tears one part from the rest, abstracts parts from the whole.' Analysis, however, is to be understood not as an ultimate, not as a goal of esthetic experience, but rather as a method, in the original sense of the word, a detour. The intuition, the first impression, cannot be held fast in its immediacy; it proceeds into reflection; then, completing a circle, reflection tends to cancel itself in a second immediacy of intuition.

Analysis, according to Herder a 'scientific' esthetics in contrast to 'natural' esthetics, is open to the suspicion that it distorts or empties the impressions that it tries to penetrate, as it grasps and defines their content. Esthetic experiences, happening to a listener in the moment of self-forgetting musical intuition, seem to elude formulation as judgments in which reflection is recorded. In art, and not only in art, received opinion is inclined to be hostile toward intellect, which disturbs any enjoyment lacking concepts. What intellect may grasp is thought to be a pale shadow of what was presented in original experience.

But a prejudice against analysis, a judgment that transforming immediate impressions into reflected impressions represents impoverishment and exploitation, might be countered by pointing out that the prejudice itself depends on reflection. Original intuition knows nothing about itself. An image of it, an idea of esthetic pleasure, which is 'sensuous, hence vital, hence thorough, hence rapturous,' is contributed by reflection. And it would not be paranoid to suspect that the lost immediacy – the condition longed for nostalgically by a culture surfeited with itself and denouncing itself – was more likely partial, musty, and embarrassed than so rich in hidden nuclear content as the goal painted by nostalgic longing. True immediacy is not the first one – the lost paradise that was no such thing – but rather the second, mediated by reflection. 'The original jet' (*Ursprung*), to borrow the words of Karl Kraus, is 'the goal,' not the beginning.

Esthetic reflection terminates in criticism. Can a theory of criticism be sketched? Or, at least, can it be shown that such a theory, if pains were taken with it, would be possible? An attempt to do so is crippled by the slogan that esthetic judgments are relative. This slogan is available to anyone and everyone who seeks to escape the implications of his own statements or those of others. Many people think that the relativity of criticism implies its worthlessness. And no matter how wrong the idea of the arbitrariness and relativity of esthetic judgments may be, it is still hard to refute. It is like the saying that no one can jump over his own shadow. This idea of relativity is one of those arguments, false in themselves, that become confirmed through the results of believing in them. Any criticism

that feels exposed to snide insinuations tends to become as unten-
able as popular prejudice expects it to be.

Surely one of the most damaging effects of the relativity slogan is
that it prevents or at least inhibits the forming of any self-conscious
tradition of criticism. Esthetic judgments lack coherence and continuity. Each judgment is presented as if, so to speak, it came out of
nowhere, although the assumptions underlying the judgment could
be discovered fairly easily. Since the assumptions nearly always
remain unexpressed, it is natural to suspect that they have under-
gone slight reflection, or none at all. However, what exists does not
measure what is possible. There is no obvious reason why it should
be unattainable or nonsensical to assemble individual judgments in
esthetic criticism, forming a context more or less like the context of
judgments in historical philology, where ideas proposed without
study of earlier utterances on the same topic are rebuffed or
rebuked as dilettantish, even if these ideas are accidentally ingeni-
ous.

Some may object that a survey of the development of Bach criticism or Beethoven criticism will suffice to lead to the resigned conviction that generally an esthetic judgment reveals more about the
person who judges than about the matter judged and its content.
This objection, no matter how often repeated, hits the mark only
approximately or even misses it entirely. For, in the first place, the
chaos of judgments, if it is a chaos, is not an inalterable situation.
And, in not a few instances, it is only apparent chaos, invoked by
picking examples misleadingly and by giving insufficient reflection
to the causes and meanings of the divergence among esthetic opinions. Even when real, the chaos can be explained as a result of the
absence of tradition in criticism. The lack of continuity, as mentioned, is not in the nature of criticism but rather based on the prejudice that combats and confounds it.

Secondly, skepticism toward esthetic judgments rests partly on
superficial reading. The belief that these judgments contradict
each other and cancel each other out is supposedly a well-
considered view, but in fact more often it is mean and impertinent.
A careful reader, whose concern for criticism extends beyond an interest in the mere verdict, the award of praise or blame, and
embraces the arguments and their implications, must notice that
diverging opinions almost always proceed from different assumptions and basic ideas, so that dialectical exertions are called for to
make the opinions comparable at all. Writers passing public judgments, who seem to contradict each other, are not addressing each

other in fact; the critics' dialogue, which a skeptic believes to be fruitless, has never really taken place. While it is futile, therefore, to play off differing opinions against each other, there is all the more need for discovering or constructing a system of concepts that would enable one to get behind the judgments and to relate to each other the assumptions that underlie them, in order to find out whether they can be reconciled or not. The differences that the skeptical view of criticism emphasizes and feeds on might possibly turn out to complement rather than cancel each other.

Third, can the history of Bach or Beethoven criticism be read as nothing but a shifting of prejudices that ruled past epochs, each epoch trying to free itself by polemics from the immediately preceding epoch? Anyone who comforts himself that this is the only reading is exaggerating. And indeed it is an exaggeration that does not provoke thought but cripples it. The differences between judgments are of course striking, but on the other hand a one-sided and strict taste is surely more than a weakness, remediable by judicious and comprehensive judgment about the past; rather it may even signify an advantage, namely, as precondition for clear and fruitful insights, the like of which would not have been possible in other times. Romantic criticism, out of style for several decades in the twentieth century, discovered traits in Bach or Beethoven that would have remained closed off to us if our century had had to feed entirely off its own substance. Furthermore, the truth-content, the validity, of any knowledge is largely separable from its origin. And ideas rooted in an epoch's prejudices, in what Francis Bacon classified and condemned as idols, are not always the worst ideas. If some notions have origins hidden in shadows, this should not prevent us from accepting the notions as the insights they are. Out of delight in unmasking we may needlessly reduce insights to prejudices, when the prejudices were merely conditions for the occurrence of the insights, not constituents of their content. Again, in criticism as well as in art itself, not everything is possible at all times. Our incapacity to make some of the discoveries of earlier centuries does not preclude our holding on to discoveries once achieved. We need not share the presuppositions of past epochs, nor worship their idols, in order to participate in the insights that grew out of them. And in the everyday experience that knowledge is more easily preserved than won we may establish hope for continuity in esthetic criticism.

Fourth, among critics who deserve the name and have not merely accidentally stumbled into the career, agreement over what

is essential, the ranking of works, is not so rare as might be wished
by a prejudice that pounces on contradictions in criticism so as to
be able to denounce them as signs of its absurdity. What is decisive
is not differences in taste, but rather that the level of argument be
kept up – both that of the issue itself and that of the presuppositions, depending on the issue, from which criticism argues. All the
rest is explanation. Even the conviction that a work is an esthetic
disaster – a conviction that underlay Hanslick's criticism of Wagner
– has less weight than doubt about a work's qualification to be
classed as art. Indeed, the violence of polemics testifies for, rather
than against, whatever is under discussion. Failed efforts and inno-
cuous successes provoke no zealous warnings about the doom of
art. 'Criticism of poetry,' wrote Novalis, 'is a chimera. Even to
decide whether something is poetry or not is difficult, but this is the
only possible question to be decided.' A critic's arguments reveal
the esthetic experience or culture at his disposal; to disparage these
is utterly wrong. But what makes him a critic is his ability to separate art from non-art. Deciding about a work's artistic quality presupposes, however, if it is to be valid, that the critic is aware of the
profound differences between ultimate principles to which esthetics can appeal: between esthetic ideas that are not reducible to
each other and that occasionally even enter into competition with
each other. Some work of art flawed from the point of view of perfection may be significant from the point of view of greatness. And
nothing has exposed esthetics to general contempt more than the
strained effort, dictated by insistence on system, to gather all possible specifications of works of art around the central idea of beauty,
or even to deduce them all from this idea. The futility of such an
effort, not to say its utter nonsense, remained hidden to an age
whose thinking was confined esthetically by classicistic norms and
methodologically by a hankering for systems. The conviction that
fitting into a system would guarantee or even fortify the truth of
ideas is one of those nineteenth-century Utopias that have col-
lapsed in the twentieth. No matter how high anyone may estimate
the influence of the spirit of the age, it is hardly conceivable how
people could fail to notice that esthetic ideas form no hierarchical
system, but rather coexist, heterogeneous and irreducible. The
attempt to subordinate them to a supreme idea, that of beauty, and
to conceive the differences among them as mere modifications
betrays a misunderstanding of their nature.

In order to revive and reexamine esthetic ideas that have been
dragged down in the ruin of the systems and to reflect on their

inherent problems, it is necessary to put aside annoyance and impatience almost forcibly. The language of esthetics has worn threadbare. It is hard to speak ingenuously of beauty, perfection, depth, or greatness, without mistrusting one's own vocabulary as mere rhetoric. Just pronouncing these words is enough to make us quail at their hollow sound. Still, an attempt to determine in rough outline what constitutes the difference between greatness and perfection might not be so gratuitous as it seems to those who allow big words to limit their reactions simply by embarrassment or disgust.

Describing perfection, in music just as in poetry, conjures up an image of a self-contained monad, which despite its limits symbolizes a whole world. According to Tieck, anything perfect is 'a special world in itself,' in which anything external to esthetics, any biographical or historical reminiscence, would mean a perceptible distraction. On the other hand, it seems to belong to the nature of musical greatness that it strives beyond the limits of music, of 'pure sounding,' to adopt Hegel's language. In the nineteenth century the symphonic poem posed a constant temptation to the symphony, the period's great form. And there is a connection between openness toward extraesthetic factors and the idea of a speaking subject who stands behind the work; both these are likelier with great music than with perfect music. With works of Beethoven, Wagner, or Mahler, it is quite hard, and would probably be unrewarding, to let esthetic pedantry prevent thinking of the composer's personality, even though, according to Kant's distinction, it is the intelligible subject, not the empirical subject, that seems to speak to listeners from within the music. The idea of a music history without names is rooted in classicism, whose esthetics circles around the idea of perfection, counterpole to the idea of greatness.

Musical greatness is not independent of the external scope and format of works, no matter how mundane this standard may seem at first. Within the narrow space of an Invention or a strophic song, greatness is hardly imaginable. Moreover, for greatness to be achieved it is not enough that a work combines wealth of musical forms and characters with density of manifest or latent motivic relationships. Large forms, rather, which hardly existed in music before the eighteenth century, before the full development of tonal harmony, demand of the composer an almost despotic mastery of broad expanses. Beethoven, Wagner, and Mahler exerted such mastery, sometimes not without ruthlessness toward musical detail. Hence it is no accident that the number of symphonies written in the nineteenth century is smaller than someone may suppose who assumes that the symphony was the epoch's representative instrumental form.

What was sometimes casually tossed off, music by Rossini or even Offenbach, may be perfect. But the word 'greatness,' if applied to the composer of the *Barber*, who surpasses the composer of the Grand Opera *Tell*, would be an empty panegyrical epithet. If the concept of musical greatness is employed to characterize, not merely to celebrate, then two ideas are connected with it: the idea of monumentality and the idea of difficulty, of not immediate accessibility. Pairing of these aspects is precarious: an incomparable example of success in doing so is the opening chorus of Bach's *St Matthew Passion*, while the opposite extremes are represented by, say, Handel on the monumental side and Webern on the inaccessible. Whereas perfection can degenerate into derivative exercises, greatness can degenerate into sterile monstrosity.

The principles of esthetic judgment, no less than works of art themselves, show the imprint of the epoch from which they come. They carry its signature. The idea prevailing almost undisputed in recent decades, that a work of art must be understood on its own terms and judged according to its own inner measure, which it shares with no other work, implies, if viewed historically, the decline or enervation of types and genres. Such a decline is characteristic of nineteenth-century music history. In the twentieth century's New Music, in which emancipation from types has been completed, each individual structure is as if abandoned to its own devices. It stands isolated, without reference to any scheme by which it might be constrained and supported. A composer has to create for himself, according to Stravinsky's *Poetics of music* (*Poétique musicale*, 1942), the resistances that he needs.

The principle of immanent interpretation is dialectical in itself. It represents the furthest consequences of historical method and at the same time a reversal of this method into its opposite. What nineteenth-century historicism ascribed to each epoch – 'immediate accessibility to God' – was claimed for each individual work by twentieth-century New Criticism. New Critics postulated that every trait of a work of art, from the details to their connections and to the whole that proceeds from them and includes them, can be grasped without regard for traditional types and schemes, by way of the work's own individual law of form. But this postulate, if taken to an extreme that can hardly be realized in practice, means lifting a single structure out of its historical context. Exaggerated historical thinking leads to treating individual works in a quarantine foreign to history. Whereas immanent interpretation seeks to be just to a work of art as unique, the rhetorical criticism that prevailed well into the nineteenth century was oriented to genres and their styles. An individual work was related to the type that it represented or the type from which it deviated as a typical modification. As late as 1850, music historians and theorists like Brendel and Köstlin were convinced that a genre was like an organism. To them history seemed like natural history, although made by men. Thus, they saw a genre at the peak of its development, its growth, reaching a goal preordained for it by nature. So it would be legitimate to abstract a norm from the peak of perfection represented by Palestrina's music in the history of the mass, or by Handel's works in the history of oratorio.

The fading of the theory of musical genres cleared a place for immanent interpretation – a place that genres had occupied securely since antiquity. Now this fading seems to have drawn esthetic judgment into a crisis, whose most striking indicator is uncertainty or arbitrariness of supporting arguments. In many cases, an ostensible argument is a mere paraphrase of some vague feeling for musical consistency or inconsistency, which is hard to explain and pin down in terms of composers' techniques, as was always possible for the genre-theory of earlier centuries. Yet the relation between interpretation and esthetic judgment is complex. On the one hand, the value judgment, which can hardly be imagined without comparing a given structure with others heard previously, seems to be suspended and superseded by the demand to grasp a work of art on its own terms, without presuppositions. On the other hand, let us stress the fact that a decision between art and non-art has already implicitly been made at the outset of an interpretation; when the interpretation has been carried out, it may be understood as the justification and proof of that implicit decision. Insignificant, undemanding mediocrity eludes a method that has been developed to deal with esoteric works, difficult of access; such a method finds no foothold in something banal. But what might be held against this method more seriously would be its inapplicability in the face of simple structures that are perfect despite their simplicity. Thus Hans Mersmann's argument that a musical work's susceptibility to analysis is a criterion of its value confronts an impasse with folksong and another impasse with the noble simplicity of the classics.

Does greater complexity always mean greater merit? This idea is too crude to do justice to musical reality, although it may be appro-

priate enough as a response to the tendency to denounce all complicated music as incomprehensible and to derive malicious esthetic
judgments from psychological tests in which subjects flunk any
questions about elaborate structures; a corresponding simplification in opposition to this tendency is understandable. Appealing to
a development toward greater complexity, as signifying some progress, goes far enough as a first move against self-righteous test-
makers. But beyond defensive and offensive arguments, there
seems to be solid evidence of concern to maintain a balance
between complication in one direction and simplicity in another;
such concern has prevailed in all periods, and the music of Anton
von Webern constitutes no exception. Some simple aspect – unity
of meter or limitation of chord-vocabulary – typically formed a
support and foil for complications in rhythmic detail or in
harmonic–tonal relationships. If composers themselves did not
seek a compensating simplicity that would lessen the strain of
listening to music, then it was the public that neglected one of the
aspects of tonal structure – such as harmony in Bach's works – in
order to concentrate on another – counterpoint.

Arnold Schoenberg recognized a principle of compensation or
economy as a fact of musical hearing and as a tendency effective in
the history of composition, but he rejected this principle as a factor
in esthetic judgment. Schoenberg mistrusted the middle path – 'the
only road that does not lead to Rome.' His thinking was anticlassi-
cistic. His opposing thesis, that to avoid inconsistency music must
be developed equally in all dimensions, he supported with the
indisputable fact that each of the components of tonal structure –
melody, counterpoint, harmony, and rhythm – coheres inseparably
with all the others; each aspect becomes what it is only in the manifold relations in which it appears. 'This is why,' says Schoenberg in
Style and idea (1950, pp. 40–1) 'when composers have acquired the
technique of filling one direction with content to the utmost capacity, they must do the same in the next direction, and finally in all
the directions in which music expands.' The idea of a music in
which all aspects are analogously developed and collaborate on
equal terms sounds Utopian. And the objection may be raised that
in dodecaphony, in Schoenberg's own technique of composing,
there is a lagging of harmonic development behind that of counterpoint; this objection is too readily available to be overlooked by de-
fenders of musical common sense; they have eagerly seized it when
they felt challenged and offended by Schoenberg's rigorous attitude. Still, in an attempt to make decisions based on sound

reasons, one of the standards that might well be adopted is what Schoenberg proposed: agreement among richly complicated and analogously elaborated contents 'in all directions,' though more exact explanations may require some reservations or modifications of this standard. The opposed point, the principle of economy, which offended Schoenberg's esthetic conscience, is more successful in explaining the success of musical works than in explaining their rank.

The progress from simplicity to complexity that Schoenberg meant is more than what can be read in a score. Besides the visible, tangible differentiation – a richer repertory of rhythms or chords – there is a categorically distinct differentiation, which demands of listeners that they think and connect. Moreover, a development that is actually progressive may look like a reduction in complexity. For example, by comparison with the rhythmic diversity of vocal polyphony, not yet subjected to what Wagner called the 'four-square' measure, seventeenth-century rhythms that are secured with beats and measures seem confined and impoverished. But this loss is more than counterbalanced. Whereas in the old mensural rhythm, described with some oversimplification, mere durational quantities were woven together in the contrapuntal web, the new metrical rhythm represents a system of graded weights; thus it is qualitatively more differentiated than the phase of development that it replaced. Rhythm is enriched by a category that was foreign to it in the sixteenth century, at least in art music. Something analogous is true also of tonal harmony in contrast to modal harmony. The repertory of permissible chord-successions was drastically reduced in the seventeenth century, but on the other hand connections between chords were more firmly secured by the part-writing, and harmonic coherence now stretched over longer passages, in something like the logical rigor of these 'chord-progressions.'

Two related difficulties make up a not inconsiderable part of the problem of trying to formulate esthetic principles: first, it would be arbitrary to separate individual criteria from each other; yet, secondly, it is no less difficult to give up the habit of operating with concepts that make sense even when used in isolation. By itself, the requirement that content should fill 'all directions' in agreement does not take us far. For in Schoenberg's esthetics – and speaking of an esthetics may be allowed although Schoenberg rejected the word, which his enemies had too often used against him – this standard implies that there is some resistance, against which a concern for the closest connections must persist. Only if counterpoint and harmony have attained, as it were, a degree of independence such that they pull apart from each other, only then is it a composer's merit to bring them and keep them together. Without a wealth of musical figures or themes, threatening to burst the form, all strict motivic work resembles shadow-boxing.

The standard of agreement among components, once more, needs modification, if a narrowing toward the classicistic norm is to be avoided. Some important works – Mahler's symphonies and even Bruckner's – are characterized by inconsistencies and discontinuities, and to deny their existence would be a false defense; rather, a usable theory of criticism ought to do justice to these characteristics. Categories like ambivalence, paradox, ambiguity, and irony, which have long been at home in literary criticism, ought to be so in music esthetics too. When heterogeneous features are consolidated in one work, this does not necessarily mean that the result is questionable or altogether botched. Mannerism is a style, not a lack of technique or of esthetic morality. Hence merely determining that discontinuities exist in a work means little. The problems of esthetic judgment begin only after a well-founded decision as to whether a particular discrepancy represents a fault or can be justified as a paradox. In some twelve-tone compositions there is undeniably a contradiction between traditional sonata forms or rondo forms and the dodecaphonic structure; is this merely lack of logic, resulting from inner asynchronism of the work's levels? or might the contradiction be made legitimate esthetically by an interpretation that renounces the complacent appeal to logic?

Closely connected with the ambiguity of inconsistency is the ambiguity of negativity. Some people believe that there are two groups of esthetic qualities: in the one group positive qualities that are legitimate by themselves, as isolated components, and in the other group negative qualities that need justification by a context in which they fulfill the function of contrast; they believe, in other words, that even elements, taken alone, and not just forms are graded in a hierarchy. This belief is a venerable relic of classicism. In the concept of esthetic negativity, true and false intermingle; a characteristic that defines some state of affairs merges too easily into a value judgment that distorts any understanding of the state. While a negative quality – a jagged or limping rhythm, a harsh dissonance, a shrill or hollow or thin tone-color – undeniably represents a factor of unrest, still some doubt is warranted about the conviction that the negative quality is mere accident, whose function consists in no more than being a contrasting foil or relief for the harmoniousness idolized by an esthetics conceived as philosophy of beauty. To regard a negative quality as something lesser, lower, tolerable not on its own account but only for the sake of its services to other qualities, is a classicistic prejudice. To begin with, why prefer the boredom evoked by a monotonous series of positive qualities to the opposite extreme, a surfeit from the accumulation of negative features? And secondly, negative elements represent the driving momentum in musical progress; for music to develop itself and reach far forward, instead of sticking to one spot, is part of the very essence of music just as much as the harmony which all parts of a work are supposed to fit into, according to the dogma of classicism. A negative that leads forward is positive.

Moreover, precisely the negative qualities – dissonance in the broadest sense – are decisive for intense musical expression, which has been closely associated with deviations from stylistic and technical norms ever since Monteverdi's *Lamento d'Arianna*. Something exceptional at its origin, an offense against the rules, either technical musical rules or those of prevailing taste, does not long remain what it was. There is an inner contradiction about expressiveness: it loses substance when it becomes established, and yet it must become a formula, a viable item of the vocabulary, in order to be understandable. Expressive value accrues to motives or chords often just because they stand out from their context. If a new theory of musical expression could absorb T. W. Adorno's insight that esthetic concepts without correlates in the technique of composition are empty, this theory would necessarily try to determine how to identify expressive prominence and distinguish it from two opposing things: the complementary contrast that even classicistic esthetics reckons as a part of its own repertory; and the incoherent juxtaposition of parts that marks bad music.

A further question would be under what conditions it is possible, if at all, for musical expression to maintain its meaning intact without becoming worn out through familiarity or through corrupting imitation, such as impressionism encountered in film music. And, indeed, the dialectics of what is new in music is closely connected with the dialectics of expressivity. In the realm labeled 'art music,' to distinguish it from folk music, for at least half a millennium – ever since Johannes Tinctoris, the fifteenth-century theorist – novelty has been recognized as one of the decisive criteria. This in spite of the contempt loaded onto novelty by people who despise fashion, to say nothing of insincere critics of new music who speak about fashion in order to disparage a music inaccessible to them, while they would not be slow to accept it if it really were in fashion.

The commonplace fact that familiar things are not perceived but merely registered and that preconceptions get in the way of things themselves and hinder an impartial experience has been made the point of departure for a theory of art by formalistic estheticians, especially the Russians. The center of this theory is formed by the category of novelty. Only something that is so surprising and so off-putting as to escape habitual forms of reaction can have any prospect of being perceived esthetically and advanced to the focus of a kind of contemplation that submerges itself in a phenomenon and its details, instead of categorizing it once and for all under some concept and passing by its peculiar character and content. Formalistic theory was connected with the literary practices of futurism, indeed so closely connected that formalism may be called the ideology of futurism, without thereby derogating its insights. But this connection does not prevent formalism from being able to explain and support an opposite extreme, the repossession of what is archaic. For a restoration of the remote past shares with an esthetic revolution the tendency to alienate. Both restoration and revolution, through the amazement they evoke, tend to cut loose perception from habits that prevent its being perception in the full sense of the word.

Thus a function of novelty is to make phenomena esthetically perceivable; but if this is so, then, conversely, it is true of fashion that it befogs a view of things and their meaning. Fashion suffers from an inner contradiction: it must of course evoke the appearance of novelty in order to stand out against the past, but at the same time it is compelled to establish itself at once as a convention, in the very moment when it comes to the fore; therefore fashion is always as if fleeing from itself. As a convention, however, fashion falls prey to a reductive perception, which carelessly devalues it. Such perception does not grasp a phenomenon in its individual disposition, but rather registers it as a mere badge of being up to date. The novelty of fashion is abstract. Without damage, without altering anything essential, it would be possible to exchange today's ruling fashion with yesterday's. Because of this possibility, fashion changes in sudden leaps. It is discontinuous. Its decisive feature is not its content, but the mere form of switching into something always different. Even if fashion copies something from the day before yesterday, it has no tradition, whereas, in what is truly and substantially new, tradition is always contained and transcended, even if in the form of explicit negation. Thus, Schoenberg's breakthrough into atonality occurred in opposition to tradition. By the very fact of contrasting with it, the new style feeds on tradition, even while at the same time the new goes beyond tradition. Then conservative criticism bemoans the loss of this tradition, accusing the new style of being mere fashion.

Relationships to music of the past are relevant not only historically but also esthetically. Such a relationship became a conscious linking in the nineteenth century, in the symphony as well as in opera and song. It is an aspect of the works themselves; it is part of their import to be connected with earlier works, either to confirm them or to deviate from them. The specific historical connection – for instance, that between Brahms and Beethoven or between Wagner's *Lohengrin* and Weber's *Euryanthe* – is composed into the music, as it were; the relationship will be perceived by listeners who know the tradition as the music demands. One of the typical traits of the nineteenth century is the parallel growth of an urge to ever new horizons and a consciousness of dependence on history. These extremes, indeed, did not merely exert their effects separately; they were also interlocked, especially in the work of the most important composers.

There is a widespread opinion that ranks the tenacity with which a musical work resists perishing and survives in performance or at least sticks in memory as the most decisive of all criteria that determine the work's importance. This opinion has become a commonplace, which no one doubts, least of all a public that feels pleased and assured in an awareness that it is the last court of appeal. And the more firmly rooted is the confidence in posterity's infallibility and even-handed justice, the less is anyone's inclination to investigate the forms of survival, no matter how strikingly they differ, nor to analyze the reasons why some works are preserved and others forgotten. These reasons do not invariably lie in the nature of the case, in the music's quality. To suppose that a work surviving for decades or even centuries owes this survival only to itself, its structure, and its expressive value, is a modern superstition.

Among the forms of survival sharp contrasts exist, such as can hardly be imagined any sharper. One extreme is the indestructibility of some pieces that are anonymous or have devolved into anonymity, which, like *La Paloma*, unexpectedly get to be a hundred years old without need for any restoration, whether motivated by delight in discovery or delight in commercial profit. Another extreme is a sort of literary fame that clings more to the name of a composer than to his works and remains inert acknowledgment of past historical significance. The art of Machaut, Josquin, and even Monteverdi is petrified; the attempt to revive this art beyond small circles is likely to be futile, unless remoteness in history is enjoyed as an esthetic titillation and archaic austerity is accepted as picturesque, and this means accepted by mistake and misunderstanding. Again, some remote and esoteric things are preserved and handed down for the sake of what may be called, as in the case of Gregorian chant, an institutional character that shields them from exposure to esthetic judgments. Although chant need not fear such judgments, they would in any case be irrelevant or quite secondary. And if anyone puts down a national anthem as musically botched or banal, he lays himself open to suspicion that his motive for criticizing is less esthetic sensitivity than a leaning towards anarchism.

Sometimes non-English people incline to suspect that some institutional pull is responsible for the prestige even of Edward Elgar, although they should not fail to recall that motives shade into each other imperceptibly and that an institutional motive tends to merge into esthetic feeling or to use such feeling as camouflage. Further, it is undeniable that Anton Bruckner's name is similarly limited geographically, and if this comparison upsets anyone, he becomes guilty, it would seem, of the same national prejudice of which he accuses his opponent.

An institutional basis for survival is not unlike a functional basis, even though here practical motives may prevail and passions may be weaker. Tchaikovsky's violin concerto and Dvořák's cello concerto will pass as immortal, perhaps for some decades yet, or even some centuries, until other works replace and supplant them in the functions they fulfill. Any criticism in merely esthetic or technical terms, no matter how well-founded, remains ineffective in the face of the demands of music business, in which there is a turbid mixture of practical compulsion and laziness. Only if Bartók and Berg are elevated to the standing of classics – and one might doubt whether this should be wished on them – will Tchaikovsky cease to be classical.

The fading of a work's fame does not always mean that it is played less often. Many pieces by Liszt and Grieg have nearly disappeared from symphony concert programs, but they have emigrated into another repertory, that of entertainment music, which supposes that it will gain respectability by attaching to itself the label 'high-class' and adapting and employing works whose return to the symphony concert is blocked by this very employment.

Almost no nineteenth-century composer is safe from the menace of vulgarization.

In contrast to the unsurveyable mass of what survives for institutional and functional purposes or even simply out of habit, there remains a small number of works of which it can be said that they have not only been preserved, but that they have a history, in which their meaning unfolds. In fortunate cases, this means that changes in interpretation – in musical performance and also in literature – resemble discoveries within the works and not merely new lighting cast on them from outside, somewhat like a shift in the 'spirit of the times,' that 'ghost' invoked now for a century and a half as often as it is derided.

The susceptibility of a work to different interpretations or realizations that are equally meaningful is one of the criteria that determine its rank. And no emphasis should be necessary to assure that this does not mean distortions, which are possible with any music, even the worst, in virtually unlimited numbers. An interpretation worthy 'of the name must fulfill three conditions, to state things pedantically: first, it must not depart from the text; second, it must be consistent and free of contradictions within itself; and third, it must not be utterly consumed with executing a literal reading of the work.

But to speak of an unfolding in history that gradually reveals what a work contains in itself is possible, strictly, only if the various interpretations do not simply line up beside each other unrelatedly, but rather are consciously linked in the relation that exists latently among them. Of course, in practice some interpretations are impossible to join together; in such cases a pressure toward synthesis would result in nothing but a levelling downward. But this does not preclude that in theory – and the task of theory would be to explain how extreme divergences come about – the interpretations form a context to which a new reading may be related.

Any musical practice that supposes it can forgo theory and criticism is like the intuition that is blind, according to Kant, as long as it lacks concepts. Of course it is the business of explicit criticism, not merely of an unarticulated public opinion, to formulate ever anew and incessantly the historical context into which musical works and their interpretations fit; the survival of music must, then, be maintained by deliberate choices. This is an idea that deserves to be as self-evident in the realm of music as it has long been in literature. Daily reviews, the sorting out of successes and failures, need supplementation by a criticism that interprets, that is supported by historical consciousness, and that traces the changes in a repertory and in the structure of a tradition.

But nothing would be farther from the truth than to think that the actuality of the past is discovered when the past is stylized to a prehistory of the present. Historical consciousness may be, on one side, a recall of the process that paved the way for what now exists, but on the other side the past engages our interest more when it is foreign to us than when it is quite like us. More rewarding than a search for precedents of modernity is a study of initiatives and interrupted developments that have been left aside by the history that leads up to us. And to discover in forgotten experience something that might be useful to present interests, no matter how indirectly, is not the worst of motives for a historian.

Bibliography

Adorno, Theodor W., *Ästhetische Theorie*, ed. Gretel Adorno and Rolf Tiedemann, Frankfurt, Suhrkamp Verlag, 1970.
Philosophie der neuen Musik, Frankfurt, Suhrkamp Verlag, 1949. Transl. as *Philosophy of modern music*, by Anne G. Mitchell and Wesley V. Blomster, New York, Seabury Press, London, Sheed & Ward, 1973.

Adorno's thesis about the 'tendency of the material' had a deep influence on music-esthetical thinking – and even on the practice of some composers – during the 1950s and 60s. 'Material,' as Adorno understands the idea, is no mere raw material of music but rather a substance already shaped by history, which suggests specific consequences to any composer who wants to produce nothing superfluous.

Ambros, August Wilhelm, *Die Grenzen der Musik und Poesie*, Leipzig, H. Matthes [1856] 1872. Transl. as *The boundaries of music and poetry*, by J. H. Cornell, New York, G. Schirmer, 1893. (See also Bujić, sec. 1.2)

Asaf'ev, Boris Vladimirovich, *Muzykal'naia forma kak protsess* (Musical form as process), 2 vols., Moscow, 1930, 1947. Part 2, ed. Elena M. Orlova, Moscow, 1963. German transl. D. Lehmann and E. Lippold, Berlin, 1976. English transl. James Robert Tull, with useful commentary, as dissertation at Ohio State University, 1977, available from University Microfilms, Ann Arbor, UM 77-147.

Asaf'ev's 'theory of intonation,' the most influential music-esthetic in socialist countries, represents an idea in the process of development, more than a finished, firmly outlined doctrine. It can be understood as an attempt to mediate between a dynamic concept of music inspired by Ernst Kurth and an 'esthetic of contents' adaptable to Marxism. An 'intonation,' as Asaf'ev conceives it, is both a component that motivates the musical process and also an expressive musical speech-melody. (CD)

Orlova refers to manuscripts dating back to 1925 concerning 'intonation.' Tull traces some origins of this idea in the work of earlier writers, especially Kurth and Boris Iavorskii. (WA)

Augustine (Augustinus, Aurelius), *Confessions* [330], transl. J. G. Pilkington, New York, Heritage Press, 1963; *The confessions*, eds. John Gibb, William Montgomery, Cambridge, Cambridge University Press [1908] 1927.

Batteux, Charles, *Les beaux arts réduits à un même principe*, Paris, Saillant & Nyon, Veuve Desaint, 1773. (See also le Huray and Day, p. 109.)

Baumgarten, Alexander, *Aesthetica* [1750], Hildesheim, G. Olms, 1961. (See also le Huray and Day, p. 214.)

Beardsley, Monroe C., 'History of aesthetics,' in *Encyclopedia of philosophy*, London and New York, Macmillan, 1967, vol. I, pp. 18–35.

Benjamin, Walter, *Ursprung des deutschen Trauerspiels*, Frankfurt, Suhrkamp, 1963. Transl. as *Origin of the German tragic drama*, by John Osborne, London, New Left Books, 1977.

Berg, Alban, 'Das "Opernproblem",' *Neue Musikzeitung*, XLIX (1928), pp. 285–7.

Berglinger, see Wackenroder

Bergson, Henri, *Essai sur les données immédiates de la conscience*, Paris, Alcan, 1889. Transl. as *Time and free will: an essay on the immediate data of consciousness*, by F. L. Pogson, London, Sonnenschein; Allen & Unwin; New York, Macmillan, 1910.

Berlin, Isaiah, *Vico & Herder*, New York, Viking, London, Hogarth Press, 1976.

Bimberg, Siegfried, ed., *Handbuch der Musikästhetik*, Leipzig, 1979.

This handbook represents a stage of development in Marxist music esthetics in which both traditional themes and newer tendencies in musicology are considered and brought to full value: philosophy of history, problems of value, theory of genres, and socialist realism; history of reception, communications theory, semiology, and formal analysis.

Bloch, Ernst, *Geist der Utopie* [1918], 1923 version, Frankfurt, Suhrkamp, 1964, 1971.

In Bloch's early chief work, a blend of Marxism and Messianism, the central chapter is a philosophy of music that sets in opposition the concept of ideology and the idea of Utopia: music, proposing the picture of a harmonious condition in the midst of a world torn to pieces, is not mere appearance, deluding us about reality, but rather anticipation of possible reality, an anticipation whereby the picture of what ought to be is preserved in human consciousness.

Brecht, Bertolt, 'Anmerkungen zur Oper *Aufstieg und Fall der Stadt Mahagonny*' [1929], in *Aufstieg* ... 5th edn, Berlin, Suhrkamp, 1969, pp. 83–96. Transl. by John Willett as 'The modern theatre is the epic theatre: notes to the opera *Aufstieg*...,' in his edition of *Brecht on theatre*, New York, Hill & Wang, London, Eyre & Spottiswoode, 1964, pp. 33–42.

Brelet, Gisèle, *Le temps musical*, Paris, Presses Universitaires de France, 1949.

Against the tendency to think and speak about music in terms derived from ideas of space, Brelet insists on the fact, often forgotten though never denied, that all categories of musical thought contain the feature of temporality. This protest against the 'spatialization' of time is reminiscent of Henri Bergson, but Brelet does not share his metaphysical premises.

Brendel, Karl Franz, *Geschichte der Musik* [lectures 1850, publ. Leipzig 1852], Leipzig, H. Matthes, 3rd edn, 1860, 4th edn, 1867, 7th edn, 1889.

Brendel edited the *Neue Zeitschrift für Musik* from 1845 to 1856, and taught history and esthetics at Leipzig Conservatory. (WA)

Bühler, Karl, *Die Axiomatik der Sprachwissenschaften* [1933], Frankfurt, Klostermann, 1969.

Bujić, Bojan, *Readings in the literature of music 1850–1910*, in Cambridge Readings in the Literature of Music, eds. John Stevens and Peter le Huray, Cambridge and New York, Cambridge University Press, forthcoming.

Calvisius, Seth, *Melopoiia seu melodiae condendae ratio*, Erfurt, 1592.

See Dahlhaus, 'Musiktheoretisches aus dem Nachlass des Sethus Calvisius,' in *Musikforschung*, IX (1956), p. 364, comparing a manuscript of 1586 with some printed editions. The edition of 1592, though it may not be the first, is the earliest to show results of Calvisius's reading of Zarlino. The edition of 1602, cited here, is not readily accessible. (WA)

Carter, Roy E., *Schönberg's Harmonielehre: a complete English translation with critical commentary*, University of Florida, Dissertation, 1978. See also Schoenberg below.

Cavell, Stanley, *Must we mean what we say? . . . essays*, New York, Scribner, 1969.

Cicero, Marcus Tullius, *De oratore*, Latin and English, London, Heinemann; Cambridge, Harvard University Press; 1942; with transl. by E. W. Sutton, intro. by H. Rackham.

Cooke, Deryck, *The language of music*, London, New York, Oxford University Press, 1959.

Dahlhaus, Carl, *Die Idee der absoluten Musik*, Kassel, Bärenreiter, 1978.

This recent book expounds more amply than before the important 'Idea of absolute music.' (WA)

Schönberg und andere: gesammelte Aufsätze zur Neuen Musik, Mainz, Schott, 1978.

The thirty-nine essays collected here are supplemented with an introductory essay by Hans Oesch and a complete bibliography of Dahlhaus's many more writings. (WA)

Zwischen Romantik und Moderne: vier Studien zur Musikgeschichte des späteren 19. Jahrhunderts, München, Katzbichler, 1974. Transl. as *Between Romanticism and Modernism: four studies in the music of the later 19th century*, by Mary Whittall, Berkeley, Los Angeles and London, University of California Press, 1980.

Two of these studies are especially relevant to issues treated

concisely in the present book: 'The twofold truth in Wagner's aesthe-
tics' and 'Nationalism and music.'
  Also there is the posthumous essay by Nietzsche 'Über Musik und
Wörter' (from the *Kritische Gesamtausgabe*, ed. Giorgio Colli and
Mazzino Montinari, Berlin, de Gruyter, 1972), translated as 'On
music and words,' in the appendix by Walter Kaufmann, eminent
Nietzsche scholar. (WA)

Dubos, Jean Baptiste, *Réflexions critiques sur la poésie et sur la peinture*
  [1719], transl. as *Critical reflections*, by Thomas Nugent, New York,
  AMS Press, 1978. (See also le Huray and Day, especially for the introductory page by the editors.)

Fugate, Joe K., *The psychological basis of Herder's esthetics*, The Hague,
  Mouton, 1966.

Gervinus, Georg Gottfried, *Händel und Shakespeare: Zur Ästhetik der
  Tonkunst*, Leipzig, Engelmann, 1868.

Gurney, Edmund, *The power of sound* [1880], with an introductory essay
  by Edward T. Cone, New York, Basic Books, 1966. (See also Bujić,
  secs. 2.2, 3.1.)

Halm, August, *Von zwei Kulturen der Musik*, München, G. Müller,
  1913, 3rd edn, Stuttgart, 1947.

Hanslick, Eduard, *Vom Musikalisch-Schönen*, Leipzig, Barth, 1854,
  transl. as *The beautiful in music*, by Gustav Cohen, ed. with intro. by
  Morris Weitz, New York Liberal Arts Press, 1957. (See also Bujić,
  sec. 1.1.)

Hegel, Georg Wilhelm Friedrich, *Ästhetik oder Wissenschaft des
  Schönen*, ed. F. Bassenge [1842], *Ästhetik ... Einführung von
  Georg Lukács*, 2 vols., Frankfurt, Europäische Verlagsanstalt,
  1966. Transl. as *Aesthetics: lectures on fine art*, by T. M. Knox,
  Oxford, Clarendon Press, New York, Oxford University Press, 1975.
  See M. Beardsley above. (See also le Huray and Day, pp. 339–53.)

Herder, Johann Gottfried von, *Kalligone*, Leipzig, Harthoch, 1800. Ed.
  Heinz Begenau, Weimar, Böhlaus, 1955.
    The Begenau edition is the best so far. Its index of topics is es-
  pecially valuable. Until an English translation is available, readers may
  consult a summary in Robert T. Clark, jr., *Herder: his life and thought*,
  Berkeley, University of California Press, 1955, pp. 408–12. (WA)
Sämtliche Werke, ed. Bernhard Suphan, 33 vols., Berlin, Weidmann,
  1877–1913; *Werke*, 5 vols., Stuttgart, Union, 1889–94. See I. Berlin
  and J. K. Fugate above. (See also le Huray and Day, p. 251.)

Hiller, Johann Adam, *Über die Musik und ihre Wirkungen*, Leipzig, 1781,
  transl. of Michel Chabanon's *Observations sur la musique*, Paris,
  1779. Reissued in a facsimile of the 1785 edn, Genève, 1969.
    Hiller contributed to Marpurg's *Historisch–kritische Beyträge zur
  Aufnahme der Musik*. Possibly the above title was such a contribution. Hiller's thoughts of 1754, referred to by Dahlhaus, p. 44,
  seem to be available only in Marpurg's vol. I. (WA)

Huber, Kurt, *Der Ausdruck musikalischer Elementarmotive*, Leipzig, Barth, 1923.

Musikästhetik, Ettal, Buch-Kunstverlag, 1954.

Huber's posthumously published lectures on music esthetics, whose philosophical foundation is formed by the phenomenology of Edmund Husserl, have their focus in the chapter on musical expression, which is described by Huber as an inalienable characteristic of the sounding object. Huber's experience as simultaneously musicologist, philosopher, and psychologist lends him a competence rare among music estheticians.·

Humboldt, Wilhelm von, *Über die Verschiedenheit des menschlichen Sprachbaues* [1836], transl. as *Linguistic variability and intellectual development*, by George C. Buck and Frithjof A. Raven, Florida, University of Miami Press, 1971.

Werke, 4 vols., Stuttgart, Cotta, 1960–4.

Humanist without portfolio: an anthology of the writings, ed. Marianne Cowan, Detroit, Wayne State University Press, 1963.

Husserl, Edmund, *Gesammelte Werke* . . ., The Hague, Nijhoff, 1958.

'Vorlesungen zur Phänomenologie des inneren Zeitbewusstseins,' in *Jahrbücher zur Philosophie und phänomenologische Forschung*, IX, 1928. Transl. as *The phenomenology of internal time-consciousness*, by J. S. Churchill, ed. by Martin Heidegger, Bloomington, Indiana University Press, 1964.

Hutcheson, Francis, *An inquiry into the origin of our ideas of beauty and virtue* [1726], New York, Garland Publications, London, Gregg International, 1971.

Ingarden, Roman, *Das literarische Kunstwerk* . . . [Halle, 1931; 2nd edn, 1960] 3rd edn, Tübingen, Niemeyer, 1965. Transl. by George G. Grabowicz as *The literary work of art: an investigation on the borderlines of ontology, logic, and theory of literature*, Evanston, Northwestern University Press, 1973.

O poznawaniu dziela literackiego, Lvov, 1937. Transl. and enlarged by the author as *Vom Erkennen des literarischen Kunstwerks*, Tübingen, Niemeyer, 1968. The German edition is transl. as *The cognition of the literary work of art*, by Ruth Ann Crowley and Kenneth Olson, Evanston, Northwestern University Press, 1973.

Untersuchungen zur Ontologie der Kunst: Musikwerk, Bild, Architektur, Film, Tübingen, Niemeyer, 1962.

Ingarden, a philosopher of the Husserl school, devotes a chapter of his book to music, proceeding from the problem of how a musical work's identity – beyond the differences among sounding realizations – can be made conceivable. He defines a musical work as an 'intentional' object (thus neither 'real' nor 'ideal') and as a mere 'theme,' capable of various fulfillments.

Jacob of Liège, *Speculum musicae* [ca. 1330], ed. Roger Bragard, Rome, American Institute of Musicology, 1955–73. See also Smith, F.

Joseph, 'Iacobi Leodiensis, Speculum musicae I (a commentary),' Brooklyn, Institute of Mediaeval Music [1966] (Musicological Studies, vol. XIII). Excerpts transl. by Oliver Strunk, in *Source readings in music history*, vol. I, pp. 180–90.

Kant, Immanuel, *Anthropologie in pragmatischer Hinsicht*, 2nd corrected edn, Königsberg, F. Nicolovius, 1800. Transl. as *Anthropology in pragmatic perspective*, by Mary Gregor, The Hague, Nijhoff, 1974, sec. 71, p. 114 (in German sec. 68).
Kritik der praktischen Vernunft [1788], Stuttgart, E. Klett, 1970. Transl. as *Critique of practical reason* [1879], by Lewis W. Beck, Chicago and London, University of Chicago Press, 1950.
Kritik der reinen Vernunft, Riga, Hartknoch, 1781. Transl. as *Critique of pure reason* [1881] by J. M. D. Meiklejohn, Chicago, Encyc. Brit., London, Dent, 1955.
Kritik der Urteilskraft, Berlin, Libau, 1790, ed. Gerhard Lehmann, Stuttgart, 1966. Transl. as *Critique of judgment*, by James Meredith, Oxford, Clarendon Press, 1952. (See le Huray and Day, pp. 215–29.)

Koch, Heinrich Christoph, *Versuch einer Anleitung zur Composition* [1782–93], Hildesheim, G. Olms, 1969.

Köhler, Wolfgang, *Gestalt psychology*, New York, Liveright, 1929, rev. 1947.

König, Josef, *Sein und Denken: Studien im Grenzgebiet von Logik, Ontologie und Sprachphilosophie* [1937], Tübingen, Niemeyer, 1969.

Krueger, Felix Emil, *Der Begriff des absolut Wertvollen als Grundbegriff der Moralphilosophie*, Leipzig, Teubner, 1898.
'Consonance and dissonance,' *Journal of philosophy, psychology, and scientific method*, X (1913), pp. 158–60.
Phantasie und Kunst, 2 vols., Munich, Beck, 1939.
Zur Philosophie und Psychologie der Ganzheit: Schriften . . . [1918–40], ed. Eugen Heuss, Berlin, Springer, 1953, fn. p. 86, and see also Albert Welleck, 'Felix Krueger,' transl. Tessa Byck, *Encyclopedia of philosophy*, London and New York, Macmillan, 1967, IV, pp. 366–7.

Kurth, Ernst, *Grundlagen des linearen Kontrapunkts*, Berlin, M. Hesse, 1922.
  Three monographs by Kurth, one each on Bach (counterpoint), Wagner (harmony), and Bruckner (form), were extraordinarily influential in the 1920s and 30s, not so much through their detailed analyses as through the music-esthetic premises by which the analyses are supported. Since Kurth conceives the essence of music as energy, in the spirit of Schopenhauer, he emphasizes 'linear momentum' (*Bewegungszug*) in counterpoint, and 'leading-tone tension' in harmony.

Langer, Susanne K., *Feeling and form: a theory of art developed from philosophy in a new key*, New York, Scribners, London, Routledge, 1953.

Philosophy in a new key [1942], 3rd edn, Cambridge, Mass., Harvard University Press, 1957.

In an effort to avoid both a primitive esthetics of emotion and an abstract formalism, Langer defines music as an 'uncompleted symbol': music is expressive without expressing any definite content; it 'speaks' without any possibility of naming what it says.

Reflections on art: a source book of writings by artists, critics, and philosophers, Baltimore, Johns Hopkins Press, 1958.

le Huray, Peter, and Day, James, *Music and aesthetics in the eighteenth and early-nineteenth centuries,* in the series Cambridge Readings in the Literature of Music, eds. John Stevens and Peter le Huray, Cambridge and New York, Cambridge University Press, 1981.

Lessing, Gotthold Ephraim, *Gesammelte Werke,* ed. Paul Rill, 10 vols., Berlin, Aufbau, 1968.

Laokoon, Berlin, Voss, 1766. Transl. as *Laokoon, by G. E. Lessing,* by Dorothy Reich, London, Oxford University Press, 1965.

Lippmann, Edward, *A humanistic philosophy of music,* New York, New York University Press, 1977.

Despite its title, this book is not so much the work of a philosopher aiming at system as that of a historian who can present music only in its cultural context, that is, a context shaped historically. The focus is in chapters on elements, structures, forms, genres, and styles of music.

Music and space: a study in the philosophy of music, Columbia University Dissertation, 1952.

Musical thought in ancient Greece, New York and London, Columbia University Press, 1964.

Lippmann describes – in a systematic presentation that is historical at the same time – first the Pythagorean–Platonic 'conceptions of harmony,' second the 'theories of musical ethics' of the 'Orphic movement' up to Plato, third the 'philosophy and esthetics of music' in the ancient system of education, and fourth, under the heading 'the peripatetics,' the musical thinking of Aristotle, Theophrastus, and Aristoxenus.

'The problem of musical hermeneutics: a protest and an analysis,' *Art and philosophy,* proceedings of a symposium, ed. Sidney Hook, New York University Institute of Philosophy, 7th, 1964, New York, New York University Press, 1966.

Listenius, Nicolaus, *Musica* [1537], Norimbergae 1549, facs. Berlin, M. Breslauer, 1927. Transl. as *Music,* by Albert Seay, Colorado Springs, Colorado College Music Press, 1975.

Liszt, Franz, *Gesammelte Schriften* ... 6 vols., Leipzig, Breitkopf u. Härtel, 1880–3. The essay on Berlioz, 1855, is in vol. IV, 1–102.

Marpurg, Friedrich Wilhelm, *Historisch–kritische Beyträge zur Aufnahme der Musik,* 5 vols., Leipzig, 1754–62, 1778.

Marrou, Henri-Irénée, *Traité de la musique selon l'esprit de S. Augustin,* Neuchâtel, La Baconnière, 1942.

A great historian, Marrou also wrote valuable works on music using the pen-name Henri Davenson. The short treatise combines his talents. (WA)

Mattheson, Johann, *Der vollkommene Capellmeister*, 1739, 1782, transl. as *Complete Capellmeister*, by Ernst Harris, in preparation.

Meyer, Ernst Hermann, ed., *Musik der Urgesellschaft und der frühen Klassengesellschaft*, Leipzig, Deutscher Verlag für Musik, 1977.

Meyer, Leonard B., *Emotion and meaning in music*, Chicago, University of Chicago Press, 1956.

From premises that mediate between Gestalt psychology and the psychology of learning, Meyer develops a theory of musical perception – an 'esthetic' in the original meaning of the word – that is supported at every step by concrete musical analyses and constantly keeps in view the preconditions of musical phenomena in the history of styles.

Music, the arts and ideas, Chicago and London, University of Chicago Press, 1967.

Moos, Paul, *Die Philosophie der Musik von Kant bis Eduard von Hartmann*, Stuttgart, Deutsche Verlagsanstalt, 1922.

Although Moos was not so much a historian as a dogmatist, who pronounced judgments and distributed censures from the point of view of Hartmann's 'philosophy of the unconscious,' still his book, consisting largely of quotations, is useful as a review of music-esthetic writings, some of which are remote and hard to come by.

Moritz, Karl Philipp, *Von der bildenden Nachahmung des Schönen* [1788], ed. S. Auerbach, Heilbronn, Itenninger, 1888. See Menz, Egon, *Die Schrift Karl Philipp Moritzens*, Goppingen, Kummerle, 1968.

Nägeli, Hans Georg, *Vorlesungen über Musik, mit Berücksichtigung der Dilettanten*, Stuttgart, Cotta, 1826. (See also le Huray and Day, p. 680.)

Nichelmann, Christoph, *Die Melodie nach ihrem Wesen sowohl, als nach ihren Eigenschaften*, Danzig, J. C. Schuster, 1755.

See Lee, Douglas A., *The works of Christoph Nichelmann: a thematic index*, Detroit, Information Coordinators, 1971. The introduction includes a careful consideration of Nichelmann's relation to Bach. (WA)

Nietzsche, Friedrich Wilhelm, 'Nietzsche contra Wagner [1888],' *Werke*, Berlin, W. de Gruyter, 1967. Transl. by Thomas Common in *Works*, ed. Alexander Tille, vol. XI, New York, Macmillan, 1896. (See also Bujić, secs. 2.2,4.)

Quantz, Johann Joachim, *Versuch einer Anweisung, die flûte traversiere zu spielen* [1752], 3rd edn, Breslau, Korn, 1789, facs. Kassel, Bärenreiter, 1953, p. 305. Transl. as *Essay of a guide to playing the transverse flute*, by Edward Reilly, London, Faber & Faber, New York, Schirmer Books, 1966.

Rameau, Jean-Philippe, *Code de musique pratique . . . avec nouvelles réflexions sur le principe sonore*, Paris, De l'Impr. Royale, 1760. Facs.

in *Complete theoretical writings*, ed. Erwin R. Jacobi. (See also le Huray and Day, next to last page unnumbered.)

Complete theoretical writings, ed. Erwin R. Jacobi, 6 vols., Rome, American Institute of Musicology, 1967–72.

Traité de l'harmonie reduite à ses principes naturels, Paris, De l'Impr. de J. B. C. Ballard, 1722. Facs. in *Complete theoretical writings*, ed. Erwin R. Jacobi. Transl. as *Treatise on harmony*, by Philip Gossett, New York and London, Dover Publications, 1971.

Riemann, Hugo, 'Ideen zu einer Lehre von den Tonvorstellungen,' *Jahrbuch der Musikbibliothek Peters* für 1914/15, Leipzig, 1915.

Riemann formulated the concept of 'ideas of tones' (*Tonvorstellungen*) in opposition to 'perception of tones' (*Tonempfindungen*, the topic of Hermann von Helmholtz); Riemann describes musical hearing as a formative activity of consciousness. He seeks justification for his functional theory of harmony and meter no longer in the nature of acoustic material, as he did in earlier writings, but rather in human patterns of musical thought. (See also Bujić, secs. 1.3, 3.1.)

Rochlitz, Friedrich, *Für Freunde der Tonkunst*, 4 vols., Leipzig, 1824–32, 3rd edn, Leipzig, Cnobloch, 1868. See Hans Ehinger, *Friedrich Rochlitz als Musikschriftsteller*, Nendeln, Liechtenstein, Kraus Reprint, 1976.

Rousseau, Jean Jacques, *Dictonnaire de musique* [1768], Hildesheim, G. Olms, 1969. Transl. as *Dictionary of music*, by William Waring [1779], 2nd edn, New York, A.M.S. Press, 1975. An edition to be published in Paris, Gallimard, is eagerly awaited. (See also le Huray and Day, pp. 108–11.)

Salmen, Walter, ed., *Beiträge zur Geschichte der Musikanschauung im 19. Jahrhundert*, Regensburg, G. Bosse, 1965.

The essays by various authors gathered in this volume focus on two topics: the beginnings of the Romantic music esthetics that shaped the musical thinking of the whole nineteenth century, and aspects of Wagner's work, which still pose a challenge that no esthetics can evade.

Schäfke, Rudolf, *Geschichte der Musikästhetik in Umrissen*, Berlin, 1934, Tutzing, H. Schneider, 1964.

Schäfke seeks not so much to give a comprehensive historical survey of authors and theories as to analyze particular texts as exemplary specimens of an epoch's spirit. Important features of the book are the presentation of antiquity, the indication of the connection between early Romantic metaphysics of instrumental music and Hanslick's formalism, and the elaboration of 'energetics' as a representative twentieth-century music esthetics.

Scheibe, Johann Adolf, *Critischer Musikus* [1745], Hildesheim, New York, G. Olms, 1970.

Schelling, Friedrich Wilhelm Joseph von, *Philosophie der Kunst* [1802]. Transl. as *Philosophy of art*, by A. Johnson, London, J. Chapman, 1845. (See also le Huray and Day, p. 448.)

Schering, Arnold, *Das Symbol in der Musik*, Leipzig, Koehler & Amelang, 1941.

The posthumously collected essays that were to have established a discipline of musical symbolism, prove to be essentially a theory of Baroque music, though Schering aimed at a universal hermeneutics. Not coincidentally, Schering earned gratitude by the rediscovery of the musical rhetoric of the seventeenth and eighteenth centuries.

Schilpp, Paul Arthur, ed., *The philosophy of Karl Popper*, 2 vols., La Salle, Open Court, 1974. See especially vol. I, pp. 41 ff., on music.

Schoenberg, Arnold, *Harmonielehre*, Vienna, Universal Edition, 1911, 3rd edn 1922, 1st English transl. by Robert Adams, New York, Philosophical Library, 1948.

Style and idea, New York, Philosophical Library, 1950. Enlarged edn *Style and idea: selected writings of Arnold Schoenberg*, ed Leonard Stein, with some new transl. by Leo Black, London, Faber & Faber, 1975.

Schopenhauer, Arthur, *Die Welt als Wille und Vorstellung* [1819], in *Sämtliche Werke*, ed. Paul Deussen, Munich, 1911. Transl. as *The world as will and representation*, by E. F. J. Payne, New York, Dover Publications, 1966. (See also le Huray and Day, pp. 323–30.)

Parerga und Paralipomena, ed. Julius Frauenstadt, Leipzig, F. A. Brockhaus, 1874. Transl. as *Parerga and Paralipomena* by E. F. J. Payne, Oxford, Clarendon Press, New York, Oxford University Press, 1974.

Schulz, Johann Abraham Peter, *Allgemeine Theorie der schönen Künste*, Leipzig, Weidemann, 1792–4.

Schumann, Robert, 'A symphony by Berlioz' (*Neue Zeitschrift für Musik*, 1835), transl. by E. T. Cone, in his critical score of Berlioz, *Fantastic Symphony*, New York, Norton, 1971, pp. 220–48.

Serauky, Walter, *Die musikalische Nachahmungsästhetik im Zeitraum von 1700 bis 1850*, Münster, Heliosverlag, 1929.

The object of the theories investigated by Serauky is the imitation of, first, affects; second, natural sounds; and third, speech-melodies. Serauky, borrowing from August Wilhelm Schlegel, describes the shift of principles around 1800 as a transition from the imitation of natural data (*natura naturata*) to the imitation of productive nature (*natura naturans*).

Shaftesbury, Anthony Ashley Cooper, third Earl of, *An inquiry concerning virtue, or merit...*, ed. David Walford, [Manchester] Manchester University Press, 1977. Walford collates the unauthorized edition of 1699 with the revision in Shaftesbury's classic *Characters* (1711). This slim volume is the only critical edition of Shaftesbury now accessible. Its introduction is masterly. The discussion of Beauty is in sections 49–52. German writers, including Kant and Dahlhaus, take Shaftesbury's philosophy more seriously than most English writers of the past two centuries, but musicians of every nationality can benefit from acquaintance with his works. (WA)

Sonneck, Oscar G. T., *Ein kritisch–polemisches Referat über die Musik-ästhetischen Streitfragen*, Frankfurt a.M., Gebrüder Knauer, 1897.

Spitta, Philipp, *Denkmäler deutscher Tonkunst, Die Grenzboten: Zeitschrift für Politik, Literatur und Kunst*, L11 (1893), II, pp. 16–27.

Stravinsky, Igor Fedorovich, *Poétique musicale*, Cambridge, Mass., Harvard University Press, 1942. Transl. as *Poetics of music in the form of six lessons*, by Arthur Knodel and Ingolf Dahl, New York, Vintage Books, 1956. Bilingual edition, Cambridge, Mass., Harvard University Press, 1970.

Strunk, Oliver, *Source readings in music history*, New York, Norton, 1950; 1965.

Strunk's anthology of sources, reaching from antiquity to Romanticism, from Plato and Aristotle to Wagner and Liszt, includes writings on music theory alongside those on music esthetics. The texts are supplied with introductions and footnotes in whose unobtrusive formulations are often hidden amazing historical and philological discoveries. (WA)

Sulzer, Johann Georg, *Allgemeine Theorie der schönen Künste*, Leipzig, Weidemann [1771], 4 vols. Supplement 1796.

Tatarkiewicz, Władysław, *History of aesthetics*, 3 vols., The Hague, Mouton, 1970–4.

Organized by the idea that the eighteenth-century convergence of theories of beauty and theories of art fulfilled a need that had grown throughout European civilization since antiquity, this unique book includes translations of well-chosen excerpts from many writers whose valuable thoughts on music are hard to find elsewhere. (WA)

Tinctoris, Johannes, 'Complexus effectuum musices,' in *Opera theoretica*, ed. Albert Seay, vol. II, pp. 161–70, n.p., American Institute of Musicology, 1975.

Triest, correspondent in Stettin (Szczecin), 'Bemerkungen über die Ausbildung der Tonkunst in Deutschland im 18. Jahrhundert,' in *Allgemeine musikalische Zeitung*, vol. III (1801).

Few dictionaries list Triest. His contemporary, Ernst Ludwig Gerber, tried in vain to learn facts about him for his *Neues historisch-biographisches Lexicon der Tonkünstler*, Leipzig, 1812–14. Most recently Triest is referred to as a 'musically gifted theologian ... debatably a clergyman ... among the foremost group of corresponding critics of the Rochlitz period' in Reinhold Schmitt-Thomas, *Die Entwicklung der deutschen Konzertkritik im Spiegel der Leipziger Allgemeinen musikalischen Zeitung*, Frankfurt, 1969, p. 169. (WA)

Vischer, Friedrich Theodor, *Ästhetik oder Wissenschaft des Schönen*, 3 vols. in 5, Reutlingen, Macken, 1840–57.

Vives, Juan Luis, *Collected writings*, Valencia, 1782; see Neal W. Gilbert, 'Vives,' in *Encyclopedia of philosophy*, London and New York, Macmillan, 1967.

De anima et vita, Turin, Erasmo, 1959 (Florence, 1954).

Wackenroder, Wilhelm Heinrich, *Herzensergiessungen eines kunstliebenden Klosterbruders* [1797], in Andreas Müller, ed., *Kunstanschauung der Frühromantik*, Leipzig, 1931, pp. 89–105. Transl. by Oliver Strunk in *Source readings in music history*, V, pp. 10–23. (See also le Huray and Day, pp. 248–50.)

Weisse, Christian Hermann, *System der Ästhetik* [1830], Leipzig, J. G. Findel, 1872.

> In Dahlhaus's *Idee der absoluten Musik*, p. 104, Weisse is identified as 'a marginal figure in the history of philosophy, the real apostle of a religion of art focussed on the idea of a "pure" art.' (WA)

Wellek, Albert, *Musikpsychologie und Musikästhetik*, Frankfurt a.M., Akademische Verlagsgesellschaft, 1963.

> Wellek understands his book as a 'rudiments of systematic musicology.' He proceeds from the wholistic psychology of Felix Krueger and emphasizes the expressive qualities of music. Like Ernst Kurth, Wellek distinguishes 'tone-psychology' – the psychology of phenomena of hearing – from 'music psychology,' whose object is formed by music as intellectual structure; thus 'music psychology' represents the foundation of a music esthetics supported empirically, not by speculation.

Wiora, Walter, 'Zwischen absoluter und Programmusik,' in *Festschrift Friedrich Blume zum 70. Geburtstag*, ed. Anna Amalie Abert and Wilhelm Pfannkuch, Kassel, Bärenreiter, 1963, pp. 381–8.

Index

Adam von Fulda (ca. 1440–1505), 11
Adorno, Theodor W. (1903–69), 95, 101
Aeschylus (525–456 B.C.), 66
Ambros, August Wilhelm (1816–76), 56, 61, 70
Aristotle (384–322 B.C.), 2, 5, 6, 10, 16, 36
Aron, Pietro (1480–1545), 39
Asaf'ev, Boris Vladimirovich (1884–1949), 101
Assunto, Rosario (b. 1915), 32
Augustine (Augustinus, Aurelius) (354–430), 74

Bach, Carl Philipp Emanuel (1714–88), 16, 21, 22, 27, 54
Bach, Johann Sebastian (1685–1750), 36, 54, 70, 86, 87, 90, 92
Bacon, Francis (1561–1626), 87
Bartók, Béla (1881–1945), 98
Bassenge, Friedrich (b. 1901), 11, 30, 58
Batteux, Charles (1713–80), 20–1, 26
Baumgarten, Alexander (1714–62), 2, 5–7, 34, 84
Beardsley, Monroe Curtis (b. 1915), 102
Beethoven, Ludwig van (1770–1827), 27, 29, 42, 49, 57–63, 81, 86, 87, 89, 97
Benjamin, Walter (1892–1940), 13
Berg, Alban (1885–1935), 64, 69, 98
Bergson, Henri (1859–1941), 74–5
Berlin, Isaiah (b. 1909), 102
Berlioz, Hector (1803–69), 2, 26, 61, 62, 63
Bie, Oscar (1864–1938), 65
Bimberg, Siegfried (b. 1927), 102
Bloch, Ernst (1885–1977), 15, 102
Bonaventura, Giovanni di Fidenza (1221–74), 2, 11
Brahms, Johannes (1833–97), 73, 97
Brecht, Bertolt (1898–1965), 68–9
Brelet, Gisèle (1915–73), 74, 102

Brendel, Franz (1811–68), 57–8, 62–3, 91, 103
Bruckner, Anton (1824–96), 60, 94, 98
Büchner, Friedrich Carl Christian Ludwig (1824–99), 64
Bühler, Karl (1879–1963), 18
Bujić, Bojan (b. 1937), 103

Calvisius, Seth (1556–1615), 24–5, 103
Cannabich, Johann (1731–98), 27
Carter, Roy Everett (b. 1931), 103
Cavell, Stanley (b. 1926), 103
Chopin, Fryderyk (1810–49), 15
Cicero, Marcus Tullius (106–43 B.C.), 7
Cooke, Deryck (1919–76), 103

Day, James (b. 1927), 11, 107
Dessoir, Max (1867–1947), 4
Diderot, Denis (1713–84), 38
Dubos, Jean Baptiste (1670–1742), 16, 17, 21, 26
Durante, Francisco (1684–1755), 49
Dvořák, Antonin (1841–1904), 98

Eggebrecht, Hans Heinrich (b. 1919), 21
Elgar, Edward (1857–1934), 98
Engel, Johann Jacob (1741–1802), 56–7

Fechner, Gustav Theodor (1801–87), 6
Ficino, Marcilio (1433–99), 5
Fontenelle, Bernard le Bovier (1657–1757), 24, 28
Forkel, Johann Nikolaus (1749–1818), 26, 41
Fugate, Joe K. (b. 1931), 104
Fux, Johann Joseph (1660–1741), 14

Gabrieli, Giovanni (1554–1612), 25
Georgiades, Thrasybulos G. (1907–77), 12

Gervinus, Georg Gottfried (1805–71), 30–1, 58, 59
Gluck, Christoph Willibald von (1714–87), 21, 49, 64, 65, 66
Goethe, Johann Wolfgang von (1749–1832), 59, 70
Grieg, Edvard Hagerup (1843–1907), 98
Grillparzer, Franz (1791–1872), 3, 56
Grimm, Jacob (1785–1863), 52
Gurney, Edmund (1847–88), 104

Halm, August (1869–1929), 78
Handel, Georg Friedrich (1685–1759), 90, 91
Hanslick, Eduard (1825–1904), 3, 19, 22–3, 29, 32, 50–7, 88
Hartmann, Eduard von (1842–1906), 108 *see* Moos
Hartmann, Nicolai (1882–1950), 81, 82
Haydn, Franz Joseph (1732–1809), 26, 27, 49, 60
Hegel, Georg Wilhelm Friedrich (1770–1831), vii, 5, 11, 29–30, 35, 46–9, 52, 53, 57–8, 61, 62, 67, 70–2, 89
Heine, Heinrich (1797–1856), 13, 61
Heinse, Wilhelm (1746–1803), 18, 21, 22
Herder, Johann Gottfried (1744–1803), 9–12, 21, 22, 28, 29, 70, 84–5, 104
Hiller, Johann Adam (1728–1804), 26, 104
Hindemith, Paul (1895–1963), 14n
Hoffmann, Ernst Theodor Wilhelm Amadeus (1776–1822), 2, 27, 41, 60, 63
Hrabanus Maurus (776?–856), 17
Huber, Kurt (1893–1943), 17, 19, 104
Humboldt, Wilhelm von (1767–1835), 10, 52, 105
Husserl, Edmund (1859–1938), 74, 76, 105
Hutcheson, Francis (1694–1746), 33

Ingarden, Roman (1893–1970), 75, 81–3, 105
Isidor of Seville (560?–636), 17, 18

Jacob of Liège (ca. 1260–ca. 1330), 14, 105

Josquin des Prez (1440–1521), 98

Kant, Immanuel (1724–1804), vii, 3, 4–5, 7, 8–9, 11, 15, 28, 31–8, 46, 62, 72, 89, 99
Klopstock, Friedrich Gottlieb (1724–1803), 27, 40
Koch, Heinrich Christoph (1749–1816), 25, 106
Köhler, Wolfgang (1887–1967), 50
König, Josef (1893–1947), 44
Kostlin, Heinrich Adolf (1846–1907), 91
Kraus, Karl (1874–1936), 85
Krueger, Felix Emil (1874–1948), 55, 106
Kühn, Hellmut (b. 1939), 49
Kurth, Ernst (1886–1946), 78, 80, 106

Langer, Susanne K. (b. 1895), 106
le Huray, Peter (b. 1930), 3n, 11, 107
Leibniz, Gottfried Wilhelm (1646–1716), 5
Lessing, Gotthold Ephraim (1729–81), 10, 107
Lippmann, Edward Arthur (b. 1920), 107
Listenius, Nikolai (ca. 1510–50), 10–11, 107
Liszt, Franz (1811–86), 57–63, 98
Lotti, Antonio (1667–1740), 49

Machaut, Guillaume (ca. 1300–ca. 1377), 98
Mahler, Gustav (1860–1911), 60, 89, 94
Marpurg, Friedrich Wilhelm (1718–95), 20, 26, 104, 107
Marrou, Henri-Irénée (b. 1904), 107
Mattheson, Johann (1681–1764), 23, 24–6, 108
Mei, Girolamo (1519–94), 65
Melanchthon, Philip (1497–1560), 10
Mendelssohn, Felix (1809–47), 6
Mersmann, Hans (1891–1971), 91
Meyer, Ernst Hermann (b. 1905), 108
Meyer, Leonard B. (b. 1918), 108
Meyerbeer, Giacomo (1791–1864), 67
Monteverdi, Claudio (1567–1643), 95, 98
Moos, Paul (1863–1952), 108
Moritz, Karl Philipp (1757–93), 13, 40, 108

Mozart, Wolfgang Amadeus (1756–91), 49

Nägeli, Hans Georg (1773–1836), 28–9
Nichelmann, Christoph (1717–62), 16
Nietzsche, Friedrich Wilhelm (1844–1900), vii, 45, 64–5, 66, 67, 103–4, 108
Novalis, Friedrich (1772–1801), 62, 88

Offenbach, Jacques (1819–80), 90

Palestrina, Giovanni Pierluigi da (1525–94), 49, 91
Pergolesi, Giovanni Battista (1710–36), 49
Plato (427–347 b.c.), x, 3, 4, 5, 6, 22, 39, 43–5, 107
Plotinus (204?–70?), 4, 5
Popper, Karl (b. 1902), 110 *see* Schilpp

Quantz, Johann Joachim (1697–1773), 26

Rameau, Jean-Philippe (1683–1764), 41, 108
Révész, Géza (1878–1955), 80–1
Richter, Johann Paul Friedrich (Jean Paul, 1763–1825), 3, 40
Riemann, Hugo (1849–1919), 83, 109
Rochlitz, Friedrich (1769–1842), 54, 109
Rossini, Gioacchino (1792–1868), 90
Rousseau, Jean-Jacques (1712–78), 17, 21, 24, 26, 31, 36, 40, 109

Salmen, Walter (b. 1926), 109
Schäfke, Rudolf (1895–1945), 78, 109
Scheibe, Johann Adolf (1708–76), 26
Schelling, Friedrich Wilhelm Joseph (1775–1854), 13, 38
Schering, Arnold (1877–1941), 60, 110
Schoenberg, Arnold (1874–1951), 1–2, 31, 63, 69, 92–4, 96–7, 104, 110
Schopenhauer, Arthur (1788–1860), vii, 4, 42–6, 110
Schubart, Daniel (1739–91), 21, 22, 27, 54
Schulz, Johann Abraham Peter (1739–1805), 27
Schumann, Robert (1810–56), 2–4, 56, 62, 63, 110
Serauky, Walter (1903–59), 110
Shaftesbury, Anthony Ashley Cooper, Third Earl of (1671–1713), 4, 6, 110–11
Socrates (469–399 b.c.), x, 39
Sonneck, Oscar G.T. (1873–1928), 111
Spataro, Giovanni (1458?–1541), 39
Spitta, Philipp (1841–94), 69–71
Stravinsky, Igor Feodorovich (1882–1971), 90
Strunk, Oliver (1901–80), 111
Sulzer, Johann Georg (1720–79), 6, 27

Tartini, Giuseppe (1692–1770), 26
Tatarkiewicz, Władysław (b. 1886), 111
Tchaikovsky, Piotr Ilich (1840–93), 98
Thomas Aquinas (1225?–74), 2
Tieck, Johann Ludwig (1773–1853), 60, 89
Tinctoris, Johannes (1436–1511), 18, 95, 111

Vicentino, Nicola (1511–76), 19
Vischer, Friedrich Theodor (1807–87), 30, 49–51, 53
Vives, Juan Luis (1492–1540), 16, 111

Wackenroder, Wilhelm Heinrich (1773–98), 25–6, 27, 29, 39–42, 47, 60, 112
Wagner, Richard (1813–83), 2, 21, 30, 35, 63, 64–9, 73, 76, 88, 89, 93, 97
Weber, Carl Maria von (1786–1826), 2, 60, 97
Webern, Anton von (1883–1945), 90, 92
Weill, Kurt (1900–50), 68–9
Weisse, Christian Hermann (1801–66), 29, 112
Wellek, Albert (1904–72), 79, 112
Winckelmann, Johann Joachim (1717–68), 70
Wiora, Walter (b. 1907), 60, 112
Wolff, Christian (1679–1754), 5, 7

Zarlino, Gioseffo (1517–90), 19